{Re}Finding JOY

Monika Zanardo

{Re}Finding Joy

Copyright © 2020 Monika Zanardo

ISBN 978-0-6482867-1-4 PRINT
ISBN 978-0-6482867-2-1 EPUB
ISBN 978-0-6482867-3-8 MOBI

All rights reserved. No part of this publication may be reproduced, stored in a retrieval system, or transmitted in any form or by any means-electronic, mechanical, photocopy, recording or any other—except for brief quotations in printed reviews, without the prior permission of the author.

Request for information should be addressed to: refinding.joy.book@gmail.com

All Scripture quotations are indicated.

Unless otherwise noted, all scripture taken from the New King James Version®. Copyright © 1982 by Thomas Nelson. Used by permission. All rights reserved.

Scripture quotations taken from TPT are from The Passion Translation®. Copyright © 2017, 2018 by Passion & Fire Ministries, Inc. Used by permission. All rights reserved. www.thepassiontranslation.com.

Scripture quotations taken from the Amplified® Bible (AMP), Copyright © 2015 by The Lockman Foundation. Used by permission. www.lockman.org.

Scripture quotations taken from the Amplified® Bible Classic (AMPC), Copyright © 1954, 1958, 1962, 1964, 1965, 1987 by The Lockman Foundation. Used by permission. www.lockman.org.

Scripture quotations taken from (NLT) are taken from the Holy Bible, New Living Translation, Copyright ©1996, 2004, 2015 by Tyndale House Foundation. Used by permission of Tyndale House Publishers, a Division of Tyndale House Ministries, Carol Stream, Illinois 60188. All rights reserved.

Scripture quotations taken from (ESV) are taken from The ESV® Bible (The Holy Bible, English Standard Version®), copyright © 2001 by Crossway, a publishing ministry of Good News Publishers. Used by permission. All rights reserved.

Cover Design: Samuel Zanardo
Fresh viewpoint: Josiah Zanardo
Editor: M Miles Design
Typesetting: M Miles Design
Produced and printed for the author in Australia by exlibris.com.au

Contents

Introduction 5
Why does joy matter? | The benefits of re-finding joy |
Selah: stop, connect, enjoy ... | How to create a Selah moment in your daily life

1. What is JOY? 13
It's not all roses and sunshine | Grace recognised: going deeper into joy |
The outworking of the grace of God | Receiving grace and experiencing joy |
Selah: stop, connect, enjoy ...

2. The Source of Joy 23
The Psalm of the Precious Secret | The power of Psalm 16 |
Drawing continually from the Source of Joy |
The Holy Spirit: the evidence of a life of joy | Walk in line with the Spirit |
The oil of joy | Selah: stop, connect, enjoy ...

3. The Joy of Salvation 35
Understanding the joy of salvation | Living in the joy of salvation |
Joy in fullness: spirit, soul, and body |
Reminding ourselves of the joy of salvation | Selah: stop, connect, enjoy ...

4. Joy is 'Considered' 45
Choosing the joy account | God's ways and thoughts | Leading our inner selves | It's a chain reaction of the emotional kind | Choosing a better way |
Corrie ten Boom | Elisabeth Elliot | Why consider trials as joy? | How? |
Selah: stop, connect, enjoy ...

5. Purpose Releases Joy 61
Purpose unlocks joy | Finding your sweet spot | Jesus: Our Mentor in finding joy through purpose | We are created for community | Purpose is found in the everyday journey of life | Finding purpose comes from being intentional |
Selah: stop, connect, enjoy ...

6. Gratitude Releases Joy 75
Be counterculture | Flip introspective grumpiness into meditative gratitude |
Time to get generous! | Perspective bolsters gratitude | 'Objects in the mirror are closer than they appear' | Chicken or egg? | Selah: stop, connect, enjoy ...

7. JOY Busters: Worry, Fear, Shame & Guilt 87

Joy Buster 1: Worry | Joy Buster 2: Fear | Joy Buster 3: Shame |
Joy Buster 4: Guilt | Selah: stop, connect, enjoy ...

8. JOY Busters: Comparison & Disappointment 105

Joy Buster 5: Comparison | Joy Buster 6: Disappointment |
Selah: stop, connect, enjoy ...

9. JOY Busters: Toxic Thinking, Un-forgiveness, & Bad Attitudes 123

Joy Buster 7: Toxic thinking | Joy Buster 8: Unforgiveness |
Joy Buster 9: Bad Attitudes | Selah: stop, connect, enjoy ...

10. Joy Inexpressible 139

Worship | Worship magnifies God and minimises everything else |
It's all about Jesus | The joy of the Lord is my strength |
Prayer and Meditation | The hiding place | The power of speaking in heavenly tongues | Righteousness, peace, and joy | Physically and practically speaking | Remind me again: Why does joy matter? | Jesus and His joy complete us | I want what she's having! | Thank you

Appendix. Joy in Ministry 156

Serve the Lord with joy | Serve the Lord with gladness | Ministry Joy Busters | Un-forgiveness | Comparison | Expectation | Ill-fitting yoke | Financial difficulty | Emptiness & Burnout | Spiritual attack | People pleasing | Dread and Fretting | Re-finding Joy in Ministry | Reminders

Final Words 179
Acknowledgements 180
Endnotes 182

Introduction

Have you ever had one of those seasons where you find yourself constantly saying, *'Really? Another thing? Are you kidding me? Everything that can go wrong is going wrong!'* This can become quite tiring and bring deep disappointment after what feels like forever. This book is birthed out of such a year.

A few years back, there seemed to be a wave of multiple difficult circumstances for us and our friends, colleagues, and family. It left me feeling like I had lost my joy. When you lose your joy, there are only three ways to go. You can give up. You can turn to some unhelpful techniques to cope, which I wanted to do, (and did at times), or you can fight and not allow the enemy of our souls to win the battle.

I decided giving up was not an option, nor was living a joyless life. The only option was the pursuit of re-finding my joy. I decided to see what God had to say, and embarked on a journey of discovery, searching His Word, the Bible, to see all He had to say about joy.

On that note, I would like to urge you that if you are getting stuck on any issue at all, to do a word study in the 'sword of the Spirit' (Ephesians 6:17 and Hebrews 4:12), the Word of God, the Bible. In that season of my life, loss of joy was the issue at hand, so that is what I searched.

It is easy these days with an online Bible, to do a word search and study each passage and ask God's Spirit to bring piercing and pointed revelation as you read on any issue that is challenging you.

Through my word study I found that the Word of God is sharper than a two-edged sword and will cut through to the core of what you are facing and bring God's perspective. It will divide the soul (your own mind, thoughts, and actions) from the spirit (that part of us which is filled with God's Spirit when we turn our lives over to Him).

What I found, as I searched the Bible on the topic of joy, was life changing. The Bible provides so much instruction and insight into joy and its companions, grace, peace and hope, and my intention in writing this book is to unfold these revelations for you so you may also take hold of the joy set before you.

In this book we will look at what joy is (and is not), how recognising grace, purpose and gratitude is the gateway to finding {or re-finding} joy, how the Holy Spirit is the deliverer of joy and how receiving a revelation about joy will completely transform your relationship with God and others.

To begin with, let's take a brief look at what joy is from a Biblical standpoint and what society calls joy. I started my pursuit into joy by reminding myself of the profound value of scripture and preparing my heart and mind to receive God's word.

My study on joy ended up being incorporated into a message I shared at our church entitled *'From the Prison of Glum to the Freedom of Joy'*. As I was preparing, I pondered what the opposite of joy might be.

The opposite of joy is not sadness because joy, as we will see, is not exactly the same as happiness. It's not only despair from desperate circumstances or depression, although it is that too. You don't have to be in a deep, dark pit to have a loss of joy. It can come from just struggling with general disappointment or feelings of shame, guilt, or fear. You can have a loss of joy from being sick and tired of one difficult circumstance after another. Or it can simply happen when life gets on top of you and you just can't cope.

Loss of joy can also accompany depression. I would like to say at the outset of this book, that if you are struggling with clinical depression, please seek help. I believe Jesus has the power to set people free from depression in an instant, but I also know He doesn't always choose to do that. I also believe finding joy in the Lord will be an amazing tool to assist you in living with depression. Having Jesus, the Light of the world, as your friend and joy-bringer will make a big impact and shine light into your darkness.

As well as this, you may still need other professional help and I ask you to be wise and seek help.

When I was asking God what the opposite of joy is, the word 'glum' came to mind. When I looked up the definition, I realised glum was the word that matched the opposite of joy.

What does 'glum' mean? The dictionary says it means gloomy, downcast, downhearted, dejected, dispirited, despondent, ... cast down, depressed, disappointed, disheartened, discouraged, demoralised, heavy-hearted, ... low-spirited, sad, ... miserable, woebegone, ... forlorn, ... fed up, in the doldrums, ... blue, ... down in the mouth, down in the dumps.[1]

'I'm going to put that on my life vision board #lifegoals', said no one ever—it's not really a list of adjectives we are aiming for in life! But, as we all know, life happens, and glum happens.

Why Does Joy Matter?

So, before we launch into finding {or re-finding} joy, why is it crucial to have joy, or if you feel you've lost it, to get it back? It's not only to make you feel good, although that is a bonus. Here are five reasons.

1. **Joy is an essential part of being a Christ follower.** If we are not joyful and radiating His Presence, then the world is getting the wrong idea of Jesus. People who don't know Him, often think God is some angry, old-fashioned, rule-enforcing, joy-dampening, distant man in the sky.

   Nothing could be further from the truth. The God of the Bible is a 'slow to anger', gracious, relational, loving, perfect Father who offers abundant life, peace, and joy to all who are willing to receive (Psalm 145:8).

2. **Joy is a third of the Kingdom of God!**

   '... righteousness and peace and joy in the Holy Spirit.'
   —*Romans 14:17*

So if God's rule and reign is present in our lives, His righteousness, peace, and joy is clear.

3. **Lack of joy puts us in a rut.** If the enemy of our souls, the devil, can steal our joy, he can get to our health, our behaviour, our thinking, and our relationship with Jesus.

When he steals our joy, it is too easy to enter a 'rut', where we lack motivation for the self-discipline required to eat well, exercise and manage our time well. The 'rut' affects the time we spend feeding ourselves with the Word of God and spending time in the Presence of God. This affects how we think, which in turn affects how we live our life. It goes without saying, then, that having the joy of the Lord in our lives is crucial to our overall wellbeing. And the enemy does not want us to thrive (3 John 1:2).

4. **Joy is our strength.** Nehemiah 8:10 says, 'The joy of the Lord is your strength.' It is important to be strong so we can fully run the race of life God has purposed for us to run, so at the end of our life we can join the apostle Paul in saying, 'I have fought the good fight, I have finished the race, I have kept the faith.' 2 Timothy 4:7.

Without the strength that comes from the Lord's joy, we lag in our race; we compare ourselves with other peoples' races and we get spiritually tired and thirsty.

5. **It is the will of God to be joyful always.** 1 Thessalonians 5:16-18 says, 'Always be joyful. Never stop praying. Be thankful in all circumstances, for this is God's will for you who belong to Christ Jesus.' [NLT]

A common prayer and question is, *'What is God's will for my life?'* Here is the answer: be joyful always and pray and give thanks in every and any season. Simple in theory, not so simple to carry out.

The benefits of re-finding joy

As I studied, meditated on, and applied what God had to say about joy in His Word, I asked others to pray for me and I spent time in the Presence of God where there is fullness of joy (Psalm 16—we will look at this later).

I am pleased to say that over time, my joy returned. I felt strengthened by God's joy, even though some circumstances did not change.

I am thankful I took a journey into rediscovering joy when I did, as a few years later I had an even more difficult, draining, and busy year. I was able to complete that year with my joy intact and with the joy of the Lord giving me strength, even though it was a hectic and tumultuous year.

I want to encourage you to seek God for all He wants to say to you and transform in you *when life is going well*. This sets you up for when storms come your way, which are inevitable, and helps you weather each one. God knows the end from the beginning, and He knows you better than you know yourself. If you ask Him, He is well able to prepare you in advance for what He knows is to come.

My prayer is that we can journey together throughout this book and that you will find (or re-find) a deep joy that will carry you through all that life brings and that you will discover the joy from the Lord that sustains and strengthens you, releasing you into all you were created to be and do.

Selah: stop, connect, enjoy ...

My husband wrote a timely and insightful book *'Finding Issachar: Wisdom and Know-How in Uncertain Times'*[2] and at the end of each chapter, he had a 'Time for Selah'. I thought I would steal the idea because I like it and because, as his wife, I can!

In the book of Psalms, you will see the word Selah in the text. It means something like 'stop, connect, enjoy'. At the end of every chapter of this book you will be have an opportunity to 'Selah'. So, grab a cuppa and find a quiet place where you can take this time and gain the most out of it.

I recommend you use the Selah moments whilst reading this book, but also to make a life habit of the practice in your everyday life as spending time with God transforms our hearts and minds as we dwell in His presence.

Ponder on 1 Thessalonians 5:16-18, which says,

> *'Always be joyful. Never stop praying. Be thankful in all circumstances, for this is God's will for you who belong to Christ Jesus.'* [NLT]

We often want to know, 'What is God's will for my life?' Could following His plan each day in this way be the answer to finding God's will for our lives in the larger questions of life? If every day we are thankful to God and pray and choose His joy, then every day, with each step, He will be leading us along His paths and purposes for our life.

How to create a Selah moment in your daily life

Ask God to fill you with His joy and Holy Spirit and yield yourself to His will.

Every day list as many reasons as you can for why you are thankful to God, different reasons each day.

Pray:

What is Your will for me today?
- Pray for others in your world.
- Pray for the world.
- Pray the Lord's Prayer (see below) in your own paraphrase, expanding it into your own personal words to your loving Father in heaven.

'Our Father in heaven,
hallowed be Your name.
Your kingdom come.
Your will be done
on earth as it is in heaven.
Give us this day our daily bread.
and forgive us our debts,
as we forgive our debtors.
and do not lead us into temptation,
but deliver us from the evil one.
For Yours is the kingdom and the
power and the glory forever.
Amen.'—Matthew 6:9-13

1. What is JOY?

Joy means so many different things to so many people it is practically indescribable, but let's have a go at describing it, anyway. Perhaps in an entire chapter we can get somewhere to explaining a little of what joy is!

Let's begin by examining how our society views joy. Companies, such as Audi and Pepsi have attempted to define joy. Audi says *'Jooooy'* finally has meaning if you own an Audi', and perhaps 'if I drink Pepsi I will have joy'.

Cadbury says, if I eat their chocolate *'I will #unwrapjoy'*. Well, I must admit, it does come close. In fact, studies have shown that chocolate releases endorphins and serotonin[3] which create a sense of feeling happy! Sorry to be a buzzkill, but as you'll soon discover, this isn't genuine joy—it's just a moment in time where your brain and body feel a sense of delight.

Advertisers use the word joy here to represent a feeling of elation, happiness, contentment—but is it really joy? It is common in modern thinking to pursue happiness at all costs and be happy all the time; that everything must go well and it if doesn't we should do whatever it takes to make ourselves happy. Happiness is driven by circumstance.

Advertising 'joy' is really just a sense of temporary happiness; however, the Bible's 'joy' is the real deal.

Biblical happiness and joy are present in our life *despite* our circumstances and are due to our position in the Kingdom of God. This is in contrast to how the world sees joy; a temporal expression of elation or contentment.

Here's what Jesus says:

> *'And solemnly lifting up His eyes on His disciples, He said: Blessed (happy—with life-joy and satisfaction in God's favour and salvation, apart from your outward condition—and to be envied) are you poor*

and lowly and afflicted (destitute of wealth, influence, position, and honour), for the kingdom of God is yours!'—Luke 6:20 (AMPC)

To summarise, a contemporary understanding of happiness is that 'happiness' waits for external things to 'happen'. It is circumstantial and conditional, and we see this play out in many situations in our lives. Here are a few common mindsets around joy that are based on an 'if this, then that' mentality:

- I will have joy when or if something happens.
- When I have more money, I'll be happy.
- When I get married or have a baby, then I'll find joy.
- When I get my own house, then I'll be happy, and so on.

Compare this with the fact that Biblical joy is an internal matter, regardless of what might be 'happening' at the time.

C. S. Lewis contrasts joy, happiness and pleasure in his life story *'Surprised by Joy: The Shape of My Early Life'*[4] and his description shows how vast joy is and how any attempt at a definition falls short.

> *'... an unsatisfied desire which is itself more desirable than any other satisfaction. I call it joy, which is here a technical term and must be sharply distinguished both from Happiness and Pleasure. Joy (in my sense) has indeed one characteristic, and one only, in common with them; the fact that anyone who has experienced it will want it again ... I doubt whether anyone who has tasted it would ever, if both were in his power, exchange it for all the pleasures in the world. But then joy is never in our power and Pleasure often is.'*

It's not all roses and sunshine

Now we all know that sometimes our 'happenings' aren't very 'happy happenings'. The Bible and life experience both tell us that things won't always go well. Jesus told us that in this world we will have trials and sorrow.

> *'I have told you all this so that you may have peace in me. Here on earth you will have many trials and sorrows. But take heart because I have overcome the world.'*—John 16:33 (NLT)

At the time of writing this chapter, the world has come into turmoil with the COVID-19 coronavirus changing our world in ways we were not prepared for. The entire world has been in lockdown for some time. People are struggling with fear, isolation, and a 'new normal' with no idea of how long it will last. Many are struggling with the disease and many more dealing with grief as COVID-19 robs them of family and friends.

Yet despite the chaos, fear, and confusion in the tough seasons, the Bible is full of promises of joy: joy inexpressible, pure joy in hardships, and so on. This is great news! Joy does not depend on what happens but can be present without happy circumstances.

At the same time, it is important to remember what joy is **not**:

- Joy is not sweeping everything under the carpet and not processing the issues.
- Joy is not pretending everything is OK when it's not.
- Joy is not a mask to cover up actual issues such as depression, grief, anxiety, loss of income, and so on. As I said earlier, if you struggle with depression, it may be wise to seek professional assistance.

Grace recognised: going deeper into joy

As we discover what joy is, we find there is a mysterious and exciting link between joy and grace. Let's take a look.

The Biblical Greek word for joy used in the New Testament is *'chara'*[5] which means: the awareness of God's grace, favour ...' or simply put, 'grace recognised'.

Isn't that a beautiful and powerful concept? Wow! Grace recognised! I could almost stop writing now because what else do we need but to recognise God's amazing grace? That alone will bring joy!

Grace is always present and available to us. It's when we recognise God's grace, and become aware of it, that we find joy.

The word 'grace' is rich and has endless meaning for us with boundless applications. It comes from the deep revelation of how far we were from God, how He met us with His love and redemption, and that we receive it as a free gift.

> *'But now the righteousness of God has been manifested apart from the law, although the Law and the Prophets bear witness to it—the righteousness of God through faith in Jesus Christ for all who believe. For there is no distinction, for all have sinned and fall short of the glory of God, and are justified by his grace as a gift, through the redemption that is in Christ Jesus, whom God put forward as a propitiation by his blood, to be received by faith. This was to show God's righteousness, because in his divine forbearance he had passed over former sins.'—Romans 3:21-25 (ESV)*

When we recognise how deep into the kingdom of darkness we were without Him, going our own way, we understand grace a little more. When we recognise we were without the love and salvation and guidance of our gracious and loving Father God and how lost we were, His grace is apparent. When we recognise how found we are through the death and resurrection of our Redeemer King, Jesus Christ, His joy, and peace overwhelm our soul.

The outworking of this gift is experienced as joy, peace, fullness and a complete filling of that spiritual hole and hunger in the depths of our being that every human feels.

Here we are talking about the eternal God who created the universe who exists without any context or beginning or end, who identifies Himself as 'I AM' (Exodus 3:14). This is the God who is defined as all-mighty (Revelation 11:17), so full of power He is able to resurrect the dead (1 Corinthians 6:14) and knows all things (1 John 3:20). This same God also loves us so deeply and personally that He sent His only Son, Jesus Christ, to live the perfect life that we are not able to live.

Not only that, but Jesus Christ took the punishment for our wrongdoing by dying a cruel death on the cross.

> *'For God so loved the world that He gave His only begotten Son, that whoever believes in Him should not perish but have everlasting life.'—John 3:16*

This same God then powerfully raised Jesus from the dead and, after being seen by hundreds of people, ascended back to heaven. He now rules and reigns in victory over sin, death and the enemy of our souls, Satan.

The outworking of the grace of God

When this grace is recognised, it releases a deep joy and peace.

I love to follow word trails, finding profound revelations as I seek to understand more, and the word grace has not disappointed in providing opportunities to explore it more deeply. I would say we need another whole book to tap into it!

Here is one passage that, for me, epitomises what grace is.

> *'But God, who is rich in mercy, because of His great love with which He loved us, even when we were dead in trespasses, made us alive together with Christ (by grace you have been saved), and raised us up together, and made us sit together in the heavenly places in Christ Jesus, that in the ages to come He might show the exceeding riches of His grace in His kindness toward us in Christ Jesus. For by grace you have been saved through faith, and that not of yourselves; it is the gift of God, not of works, lest anyone should boast. For we are His workmanship, created in Christ Jesus for good works, which God prepared beforehand that we should walk in them.'—Ephesians 2:4-10*

Grace is further defined by James Ryle, Pastor, conference speaker, President of Truthworks and Founder of Promise Keepers:

> *'Grace is the empowering Presence of God enabling you to be who He created you to be, and to do what He has called you to do.'*[6]

So, grace is a free gift to us, through God's love and mercy, that saves us from sin and death and then empowers us to walk in all God created us to walk in.

You probably know the words from the famous hymn *'Amazing Grace'*. A few years back, songwriter Chris Tomlin added a bridge to the song, and the words depict some of the joy that comes from this amazing grace we are invited to encounter.

> *'My chains are gone,*
> *I've been set free,*
> *My God, my Saviour*
> *Has ransomed me*
> *And like a flood,*
> *His mercy reigns,*
> *Unending love,*
> *Amazing grace!'*[7]

There is no better news—to receive what we don't deserve and to be set free and empowered!

Receiving grace and experiencing joy

Let's go back to our joy definition, from the Greek word for joy: *chara*, meaning grace recognised. Joy comes then, when we are aware of and recognise the 'exceeding riches' of God's grace towards us and all He has created us to be and do.

How then do we recognise grace? Since it is a free gift, we recognise it by receiving it and seeking to learn what it means to walk in what we have received. This revelation is revealed to us by God's Holy Spirit.

> *'Yet to us God has unveiled and revealed them by and through His Spirit, for the [Holy] Spirit searches diligently, exploring and examining everything, even sounding the profound and bottomless things*

of God [the divine counsels and things hidden and beyond man's scrutiny]. Now we have not received the spirit [that belongs to] the world, but the [Holy] Spirit who is from God, [given to us] that we might realise and comprehend and appreciate the gifts [of divine favour and blessing so freely and lavishly] bestowed on us by God.'—1 Corinthians 2:10, 12 (AMPC)

When we ask God to fill our spirit with the Holy Spirit, it is like a veil is lifted off our hearts and minds. With the veil gone, we can understand some of the deep mysteries of God's amazing grace.

If you have not done this yet, why don't you speak to God and tell Him you would like to receive His Spirit. Invite Holy Spirit to fill you completely, to dwell in your spirit and to illuminate the mysteries of God so they are a deep heart revelation.

This passage continues, explaining that without the Holy Spirit, we reject the revelations of God's Spirit because they don't make any sense to our human thinking without the illumination of the Spirit.

There is no end to defining joy, but I have found a few rich definitions worth considering.

Oswald Chambers (early 20th century preacher, evangelist, Bible college principal) says—

> *Joy is the great note all through the Bible. We have the notion of joy that arises from good spirits or good health, but the miracle of joy of God has nothing to do with a man's life or his circumstances or the condition he is in. Jesus Christ does not come to a man and say, 'Cheer up.' He plants within a man the miracle of the joy of God's own nature.*[8]

Mother Teresa defines it as—

> *Joy is prayer; joy is strength: joy is love; joy is a net of love by which you can catch souls.*[9]

The old song I sang growing up, *Joy is the Flag*, describes joy as a flag flown high in the castle of my heart when the King is in residence there. It's a funny old song but has a lot of truth in it. When Jesus is King of our lives, joy is released.

Most people think the opposite: *If I turn my life over to Jesus, He will take away all the fun.* Not true. He releases the joy that runs deep. He may take away some of the empty ways by which we may try to access joy, but these leave us wanting: addictions that feel good at the time but leave an emptiness craving more and more, success and money which we can never get enough of to satisfy, relationships which will always disappoint, even the best ones, leaving us feeling lonely.

There are so many definitions of joy available. Here is one I came up with about what joy means for me:

> *It's like a supernatural ability to be positive instead of negative and to be contented no matter what else is going on. It is an excitement and assurance of His salvation and Presence. It's energy—He says the joy of the Lord is my Strength so when I ask for His joy, I have more strength and energy. It's like a deep connection in my spirit with Holy Spirit that produces security and peace and a 'knowing' of being loved. It is a supernatural strength to go beyond me, to go beyond what I naturally have the capacity for.*

I pray this definition speaks to you and encourages you. I encourage you to ask Jesus for His joy and see what the joy He gives is like. You can then develop your own definition and share it with those around you to spread the joy!

Selah: stop, connect, enjoy ...

Quietly sit in His presence. Ask Jesus to fill you with His Spirit, joy, and grace. Invite Holy Spirit to fill you and unveil the profound realities of God's grace.

If part of the meaning of joy is 'grace recognised', how can you recognise grace in deeper and more personal ways? Ask Jesus to bring deeper revelation to you about His amazing grace.

If you aren't familiar with the grace I have been speaking of in this chapter, here are some beautiful descriptions from author Max Lucado.[10]

> *'Grace is everything Jesus. Grace lives because he does, works because he works, and matters because he matters. He placed a term limit on sin and danced a victory jig in a graveyard. To be saved by grace is to be saved by him—not by an idea, doctrine, creed, or church membership, but by Jesus himself, who will sweep into heaven anyone who so much as gives him the nod.*
>
> *Grace is God as heart surgeon, cracking open your chest, removing your heart—poisoned as it is with pride and pain—and replacing it with his own. Rather than tell you to change, he creates the change. Do you clean up so he can accept you? No, he accepts you and begins cleaning you up. His dream isn't just to get you into heaven but to get heaven into you.*
>
> *To live as God's child is to know, at this very instant, that you are loved by your Maker not because you try to please him and succeed, or fail to please him and apologise, but because he wants to be your Father. Nothing more. All your efforts to win his affection are unnecessary. All your fears of losing his affection are needless. You can no more make him want you than you can convince him to abandon you. The adoption is irreversible. You have a place at his table.*

If you would like to receive this grace, here is an example of what you can pray:

'Lord Jesus Christ, I am sorry for the things I have done wrong in my life (take a few moments to ask his forgiveness for anything particular that is on your conscience).

Please forgive me and thank you that you accept me. I now turn from everything that I know is wrong.

Thank you, that you died on the cross for me, so that I could be forgiven and set free.

Thank you, that you offer me forgiveness and the free gift of your Spirit. I now receive that gift.

Please come into my life by your Holy Spirit to be with me forever. Thank you Lord Jesus, Amen."[11]

2. The Source of Joy

My forage through the Bible for joy revealed some treasured and, at times, surprising discoveries. As I convey my findings, I think the source is *a very good place to start*. If we are to find {or re-find} anything, we need to know where it is.

It may come as no surprise, then, when I tell you the source of joy is God: God the Father, God the Son (Jesus), and God the Holy Spirit.

So, if the source of joy is the Lord, it makes sense that the more time we spend in the presence of God the more joy we encounter.

This is a simple yet mysterious truth. Theoretically this appears to be a simple process. On a practical level, however, it is often hard to live out. Our lives are busy and there is always something else we could be doing. Additionally, we have an enemy of our souls, the devil who wishes to rob and steal our joy, and will do anything to tempt us away from God's Presence.

> *'The thief does not come except to steal, and to kill, and to destroy. I have come that they may have life, and that they may have it more abundantly.'*—John 10:10

Our minds can believe guilt or shame-based lies that we are not worthy to be in the Presence of a Holy God. Our thoughts can take us to worry, fear, despair and disappointment and hold us captive in those dark places, instead of going to the source of light and joy with our pain and anxieties.

The Psalm of the Precious Secret

Psalm 16 tells us that we find joy in His presence. Not just a small portion or a 'half-joy'. No, it says in His presence there is fullness of joy to be found.

> *'You will show me the path of life; in Your presence is fullness of joy; at Your right hand are pleasures forevermore.'—Psalm 16:11*

This Psalm is referred to in the New Testament in Acts 2 following Jesus' death, resurrection, and ascension back to heaven. Peter and the disciples encountered the Holy Spirit and Pentecost was the resulting encounter, revealing the power of the Holy Spirit for each individual.

On this day, now known as Pentecost, people gathered in Jerusalem from many nations and were amazed at the outpouring of the Holy Spirit accompanied by the gift of tongues. They each heard the wonderful news of what God has done in their own language, despite the fact that the disciples were all from Galilee. Some genuinely thought the disciples were drunk. The apostle Peter stands up and speaks to the crowd and explains that what is happening was prophesied long ago.

> *'People of Israel, listen! God publicly endorsed Jesus the Nazarene by doing powerful miracles, wonders, and signs through him, as you well know. But God knew what would happen, and his prearranged plan was carried out when Jesus was betrayed. With the help of lawless Gentiles, you nailed him to a cross and killed him. But God released him from the horrors of death and raised him back to life, for death could not keep him in its grip. King David said this about him:*
>
> *'I see that the Lord is always with me. I will not be shaken, for he is right beside me. No wonder my heart is glad, and my tongue shouts his praises! My body rests in hope. For you will not leave my soul among the dead or allow your Holy One to rot in the grave. You have shown me the way of life, and you will fill me with the joy of your presence.'—Acts 2:22-28 (NLT)*

As part of his address, Peter references Psalm 16 and declares that David was prophetically referring to Jesus when He spoke of 'Lord' in this Psalm. Jesus is the only One who would experience resurrection life. Jesus is the only One who shows the way of life. Jesus is the only One who would fill His people with joy!

The power of Psalm 16

> *'Joy doesn't come from success, circumstances, or a lack of adversity. It's a gift that comes from spending time with the One who created it.'*—Christine Caine

Psalm 16 begins with the word 'Michtam'. Commentators around the world have given this psalm various designations including 'The Psalm of the Precious Secret'[12], 'David's Jewel' and 'The Golden Psalm'[13].

Imagine this for a moment: an invitation into a secret garden with golden beams of light shining through the clouds where precious jewels of life and joy are found. I like the sound of that, don't you? We have access to a golden, precious secret jewel!

Personally, I love this whole Psalm and it has spoken to me in so many ways over the years. Here it is from verse five in the Amplified version which magnifies the depth of meaning by expanding on the original Hebrew words.

> *'The Lord is the portion of my inheritance, my cup [He is all I need]; You support my lot. The [boundary] lines [of the land] have fallen for me in pleasant places; indeed, my heritage is beautiful to me. I will bless the Lord who has counselled me; indeed, my heart (mind) instructs me in the night. I have set the Lord continually before me; because He is at my right hand, I will not be shaken. Therefore, my heart is glad and my glory [my innermost self] rejoices; my body too will dwell [confidently] in safety, for You will not abandon me to Sheol (the nether world, the place of the dead),nor will You allow Your Holy One to undergo decay. You will show me the path of life; in Your presence is fullness of joy; in Your right hand there are pleasures forevermore.'*—Psalm 16:5-11 (AMP)

Drawing continually from the Source of Joy

I love the fact that Jesus is my portion; in other words my lot in life. No matter what else is happening, my portion is that I can know Jesus and know He is with me. I love that I can freely, without any barriers, go to the Source of joy and life. I love that I can spend time in meditation and prayer with Jesus and be in the place of His Presence, where He releases joy into my spirit and soul.

I have just had a break from writing. After starting this book, a close friend of mine lost their joy and whilst supporting them, I found it difficult to write about joy.

But upon reviewing this chapter as I returned to writing, it reminded me of how much the concept of joy is about Jesus, that joy is found in Jesus as the source and reason for joy. I realised that regardless what is going on around me, joy is constant when I am intentionally positioning myself in the presence of God and seeking his revelation for my life.

My husband wrote about the curved balls of life in his book about wisdom. There are certainly curved balls thrown at all of us throughout our lives. Those curved balls rob our joy. Those are the times to be drawing from the Source.

> *'It is so very dangerous to adopt the revelation of others. It can help, encourage, and build faith but we must discover and know God for ourselves. This is where wisdom and understanding is birthed. This is the genesis of Kingdom biblical wisdom and application in life's curved balls: at the feet of Jesus.'*[14]

It must be a continual revelation, a persistent going back into His Presence, drawing continually from the source of joy. But does God have enough joy to give us? Yes! He is enough—He has unlimited joy for anyone who asks for it—it's us who forget the source. Life happens, 'poop' hits the fan. And it is easy to forget that we have an enemy ready to pounce and destroy any joy we have experienced in God's presence and partake in the abundant life Jesus came to gift us with (John 10:10).

When it comes to our joy, we need to be 'on guard', in the stance of agility of heart in the Presence of our Lord. My Dad was in the Rome and Melbourne Olympic Games for Fencing, and gave me lessons as I was growing up. He always started with the words 'on guard', which meant to move into a stance with knees bent and agile ready to move backward or forward, with the sword raised 'at the ready'. As Ephesians 6:10-12 and 16-17 state, we need to guard our joy from the enemy who will try to steal it and have our swords 'at the ready'.

I admire how the theologians from years ago wrote so poetically regarding Psalm 16. In Charles Spurgeon's *'The Treasury of David' Bible Commentary*, he quotes his contemporary, theologian John Trapp, who writes—

> *'Here is as much said as can be, but words are too weak to utter it. For quality there is in heaven joy and pleasures; for quantity, a fullness, a torrent whereat they drink without let or loathing; for constancy, it is at God's right hand, who is stronger than all, neither can any take us out of his hand; it is a constant happiness without intermission: and for perpetuity it is for evermore. Heaven's joys are without measure, mixture, or end.'*[15]

Isn't that glorious? Through Jesus, we have access to the supply of joy that has no measure or end!

How do we access that unlimited supply? I looked up synonyms for unlimited and one is bottomless. Have you ever been to a café and they offer bottomless coffee? How do you get it? It's not like the waiter gives you a cup that has built into it a supply that automatically makes your cup fill up with coffee. Now there's a clever invention for someone to figure out, although I think we'd all be a bit highly strung from all that coffee! No, we need to have the waiter near us and ask him to fill it. The coffee is still bottomless, but we need proximity to the waiter to have it filled and we need to ask him for more.

Jesus instructs us to keep on asking, and we will receive abundant joy. He says to keep asking Him, so our cup is full of His joy. Unlike a café who eventually would run out of coffee beans, if we went crazy and drank coffee all day, His joy actually is bottomless and endless.

> *'Until now you have not asked [the Father] for anything in My name; but now ask and keep on asking and you will receive, so that your joy may be full and complete.'—John 16:24 (AMP)*

Why don't you take a moment right now and ask Jesus to fill you with joy?

The Holy Spirit: the evidence of a life of joy

I find it extremely reassuring that when Jesus left this earth to go back to heaven, He did not leave us alone to fend for ourselves. He did not leave us as an orphan with no sense of place or home. He left us with His Spirit to inhabit our spirit.

The Bible tells us in Galatians that joy is a fruit or an evidence of the Holy Spirit living in us.

> *'But the fruit of the [Holy] Spirit [the work which His presence within accomplishes] is love, joy (gladness), peace, patience (an even temper, forbearance), kindness, goodness (benevolence), faithfulness, gentleness (meekness, humility), self-control (self-restraint, continence). Against such things there is no law [that can bring a charge]. And those who belong to Christ Jesus (the Messiah) have crucified the flesh (the godless human nature) with its passions and appetites and desires. If we live by the [Holy] Spirit, let us also walk by the Spirit. [If by the Holy Spirit we have our life in God, let us go forward walking in line, our conduct controlled by the Spirit.].'—Galatians 5:22-25 (AMPC)*

Not sure about you, but I'd like to have a whole lot of all of that fruit in my life! How is this accomplished? By trying my hardest? No, that often has the opposite effect. If I try so hard to have this fruit, I end up being consumed by trying instead of loving and having joy and peace. I end up impatient with others because I am so tired trying to be perfect or frustrated with others if they don't have the fruit. No, it says this is accomplished by the work of the Holy Spirit's presence within us. So it follows, if we want more fruit, we need more of the Holy Spirit's work in us.

Jesus also talks about fruit in John 15 and He says that we need to abide in Him and He in us.

> *'Abide in Me, and I in you. As the branch cannot bear fruit of itself, unless it abides in the vine, neither can you, unless you abide in Me. I am the vine; you are the branches. He who abides in Me, and I in him, bears much fruit; for without Me you can do nothing.'—John 15:4-5*

What does abide mean? It's from the Greek word *'meno'* which is a verb and means:

> 'A primary verb; to stay (in a given place, state, relation or expectancy)—abide, continue, dwell, endure, be present, remain, stand, tarry ...'[16]

As it is a verb, it suggests that it is a doing word but the 'doing' is not trying to make fruit. A branch cannot make fruit. A branch is not even alive if it is not connected to the vine or tree. To abide is to stay continually in Him and He in us. To abide is making Jesus the place our inner being lives. To abide is inviting Him and yielding to His Spirit to be continually staying and living in us.

Nicky Gumbel, who developed the Alpha course, says—

> *'Jesus says that if you stay close to him ('remain in him') three things will happen in terms of fruitfulness. First, your prayers will be answered (v.7). Second, God will be glorified (v.8). Third, your joy will be complete and overflowing (v.11, AMP). Jesus wants you to be filled with joy and fully alive. There's no greater joy than to know you are valued, precious and loved by God and to love others as you are loved. There's no greater joy than giving eternal life to others in and with Jesus.'*[17]

I can honestly say that this has been my experience. When I abide in Him and know and accept God's love, I feel valued and, in those moments, I am fully alive in who He created me to be. I say 'in those moments' because it is a journey throughout our lives; we can only partially know His love in our humanness, as it is too deep to grasp in its fullness (Ephesians 3:19).

> An incredible sense of joy comes from knowing God's love as a deep heart revelation. This revelation of His love translates into knowing your value and worth in Him. This is the joy that makes you fully alive!

So, going back to the passage about the fruit in Galatians, what is our part in it? We are to 'crucify our flesh ' which is our godless human nature. This means we are to live in a place of surrender. It means praying for the parts of us that are godless to die, the selfish parts that have no room for God to die and asking God to fill those parts with His Spirit.

Walk in line with the Spirit

Galatians 5:25 says to 'Walk by the Spirit ... walking in line, our conduct controlled by the Spirit.' We have a dog called Prince. He is a gorgeous, black Bordoodle: Border Collie cross Labradoodle. After food and 'his humans', his next favourite thing is to go for a walk. When we say the word 'walk', his does his cute 'tilt his head to one side' thing and gets all excited. When we are on the walk, if we want him to walk alongside us, we say 'heel' and he has to walk next to us. We control his conduct.

The big difference between us and our dog is that we were created with freewill. Since God doesn't put a leash on us to make us obey, it is up to our own freewill to *decide* to obey. I'm not saying we are the Holy Spirit—a long way off! And I am certainly not saying we are dogs, but the picture of a dog walking alongside its owner as 'a man's best friend' goes a small way toward an analogy of us walking in step with the Spirit. There is much joy as dog and owner walk along together. There is not much joy if the dog runs off and gets lost!

In Ephesians 5 the Bible explores the difference between being physically drunk with wine—out of control, incapable of thinking straight, having compromised conduct—and being filled with the Holy Spirt—disciplined, wise, and filled with love, joy, peace, patience, kindness, goodness, faithfulness, gentleness and self-control.

Let's look at some of these comparisons:

- Be filled with the Holy Spirit instead of being drunk with wine.
- Let your conduct be controlled by the Holy Spirit rather than being out of control when physically drunk.

- Live under the influence of the Holy Spirit and be led by the fruit he releases in us: love, joy, peace ... etc. instead of living under the influence of alcohol.

But we often struggle to come under His influence and live in a place of right standing with Jesus, so the Holy Spirit is here to guide us and comfort us, and be the counsellor we need (John 14:16). And as we let ourselves be guided by and influenced by his presence, we experience a greater sense of freedom than any other experience could provide.

> 'Now the Lord is the Spirit, and where the Spirit of the Lord is, there is liberty (emancipation from bondage, freedom).'—2 Corinthians 3:17 (AMPC)

The oil of joy

The Bible is full of analogies that liken joy to oil poured out from the Holy Spirit. The prophecy of the ministry of Jesus in Isaiah, which is now transferred onto us by His Spirit, says that we have the ministry of releasing the oil of joy instead of mourning.

> 'To console those who mourn in Zion,
> To give them beauty for ashes,
> The oil of joy for mourning,
> The garment of praise for the spirit of heaviness;
> That they may be called trees of righteousness,
> The planting of the LORD, that He may be glorified.'
> —Isaiah 61:3 (NKJV)

What does oil do? Oil soothes chafing. Oil makes noisy, grating hinges quiet. Oil cures dryness. Oil has anti-inflammatory properties; olive oil helps heart health[18]. Just as physical oil does all of this, so the spiritual oil of the Spirit does too. His oil makes the way smooth, quietens irritating and grating, refreshes dryness, calms inflammatory situations, and helps spiritual heart health.

Cars need a regular grease and oil change. I am not in any way mechanically minded, so I googled what happens if a car does not have its regular grease and oil change. The car gets engine noise and rumbling; the oil gets dark and dirty and smelly and it can start releasing smoke[19]. Likewise, our hearts can get a little noisy and rumbly (or grumbly) and somewhat dark and smelly. We can release some smoke when our fuse becomes a bit short—not sure about you, but I need a regular grease and oil change too from Holy Spirit.

Aromatherapists tell us that rose oil can help with grief and loss. Holy Spirit oil soothes mourning and actually transforms the mourning into joy. Holy Spirit provides His empowering presence to sustain us during mourning (remember from Chapter 1 that joy is different to happiness—joy is grace recognised).

In 2018, both my parents died six months apart. We also handed over the church we had led for 18 years and made the decision to move to Melbourne from Sydney. Oh, and our youngest son finished high school, so one of my strongest identity's as mother evolved into a new season. A lot of loss and change in one year!

I am so thankful to God that He had led me on this journey of finding joy a few years before all of this. It is like He set me up for 2018 in advance to know how to draw from His joy and presence. I can honestly say His presence and joy sustained me that year. He turned what should have been deep mourning and despair into the type of joy that empowers and enables to keep walking without drowning. His joy empowered me to keep giving out to others because that was what I was called to. His Presence and comfort allowed me to cry when needed (and I am a big cry-er, so cry I did) but not sink and drown.

Now for one more reference to God being the source of joy before I close out this chapter, which is found in this amazing verse.

> *'May the God of your hope so fill you with all joy and peace in believing [through the experience of your faith] that by the power of the Holy Spirit you may abound and be overflowing (bubbling over) with hope.'—Romans 15:13 (AMPC)*

The Passion Translation (not a version but a poetic paraphrase) says it this way:

> 'Now may God, the inspiration and fountain of hope, fill you to overflowing with uncontainable joy and perfect peace as you trust in Him. And may the power of the Holy Spirit continually surround your life with his super-abundance until you radiate with hope!'—Romans 15:13 (TPT)

The God of our hope fills us with joy and peace. The mystery is that whilst we have a part to play, we do not strive to be filled with joy or peace: He fills us. We spend time with him, believe and trust in and put our faith and hope in Him and the outworking of this is the tangible and profound experience of joy and peace as we recognise and declare that he is the source of these things.

God's Spirit releases joy, fills us with joy, grows joy in us and oils us with joy. And we do well to stay close to the Source.

Selah: stop, connect, enjoy ...

Time for that grease and oil change!

Find a special quiet space, go for a walk in nature or rest under a tree. I have a hammock under a tree in my backyard and it is one of my happy places where I go and read a book or contemplate. As I lie there, I look up through the branches, and I like to meditate on John 15.

In your special quiet space, meditate on what it means to be a branch who abides/lives/dwells in Jesus and what it means to have Him abide/live/dwell in you.

> *'Abide in Me, and I in you. As the branch cannot bear fruit of itself, unless it abides in the vine, neither can you, unless you abide in Me. I am the vine; you are the branches. He who abides in Me, and I in him, bears much fruit; for without Me you can do nothing.'—John 15:4-5*

Read Psalm 16. Imagine: a secret garden with golden beams of light shining through the clouds where precious jewels of life and joy are found.

As you spend time in His presence, ask Him to release His joy into your spirit and soul.

Ponder on what it means for Jesus to be your portion. Ask Him to show you His path of life for you.

Ask God to fill you with His Spirit so His fruit grows in you and empowers you to walk in line with His Spirit.

Meditate on Romans 15:13

> *'May the God of your hope so fill you with all joy and peace in believing [through the experience of your faith] that by the power of the Holy Spirit you may abound and be overflowing (bubbling over) with hope.'*

3. The Joy of Salvation

Isaiah prophesied this joy of salvation about 700 years before Jesus came to this earth to bring salvation.

> *'Behold, God is my salvation, I will trust and not be afraid; 'For Yah, the Lord, is my strength and song; He also has become my salvation." Therefore, with joy you will draw water from the wells of salvation.*
> *—Isaiah 12:2-3*

The Barnes commentary explains the imagery of a well. 'A fountain, or a well, in the sacred writings, is an emblem of that which produces joy and refreshment; which sustains and cheers. The figure is often employed to denote that which supports and refreshes the soul; which sustains man when sinking from exhaustion, as the babbling, fountain or well refreshes the weary and fainting pilgrim.'[20]

Jesus speaks of His water in John 4:13-14 and 7:37. He gives water to our soul which quenches our thirst so completely that our soul will never thirst again. If we fill ourselves with Jesus and His Spirit as our soul thirst-quencher, we will be satisfied. How amazing is that? When we draw His water for our souls from the wells of salvation, we receive joy and strength.

Jesus answered and said to her—

> *'Whoever drinks of this water will thirst again, but whoever drinks of the water that I shall give him will never thirst. But the water that I shall give him will become in him a fountain of water springing up into everlasting life.'—John 4:13-14*

What do we need to do? Draw water. How? Go to Him as our well, with the bucket, which is our entire selves, and allow Him to fill us.

> *'On the last day, that great day of the feast, Jesus stood and cried out, saying, 'If anyone thirsts, let him come to Me and drink. He who*

believes in Me, as the Scripture has said, out of his heart will flow rivers of living water.'—John 7:37

Understanding the joy of salvation

Delicious joy! Joy unspeakable! These are the testimonies of two men who God used in mighty ways to spark revivals where thousands of people were touched by God and found the joy of salvation; their lives were changed dramatically and were never the same again.

> *'Now, there are three kinds of joy; there is the joy of one's own salvation. I thought, when I first tasted that, it was the most delicious joy I had ever known, and that I could never get beyond it. But I found, afterward, there was something more joyful that, namely, the joy of the salvation of others ... [and the third] ... the Lord gives His people perpetual joy when they walk in obedience to Him.* [21]*—DL Moody*

Struggling to achieve salvation through his own efforts, George Whitefield learnt it is through Christ we have acceptance with God. He wrote in his journal, 'God was pleased to remove the heavy load, to enable me to lay hold of his dear Son by a living faith. With what joy—joy unspeakable—was my soul filled!'[22]

I, too, have had moments of exhilarating joy with the recognition of the un-surpassing good news of salvation. We saw in Chapter 1 that joy comes from 'grace recognised'. When we recognise the grace of God as we see in John 3:16, we discover the joy of our salvation.

> *'For God so loved the world that He gave His only begotten Son, that whoever believes in Him should not perish but have everlasting life.'—John 3:16*

> *'We are writing these things to you so that our ... may be made complete [by having you share in the joy of salvation]. This is the message [of God's promised revelation] which we have heard from Him and now announce to you, that God is Light [He is holy, His message is truthful, He is perfect in righteousness], and in Him there is no darkness at all [no sin, no wickedness, no imperfection].'—1 John 1:4-5 (AMP)*

Jesus came to earth to bring us salvation, to bring light into our darkness, to bring life to our death and to be perfect in our place.

When Jesus, the eternal son of God, was conceived by the Holy Spirit and born of a virgin as a baby on our earth, the angels declared to the shepherds in the field that He would bring joy to all people.

Even heaven has joy when it comes to salvation. When a person accepts the salvation of Jesus, the angels and God in heaven celebrate with great joy.

> *'And when he comes home, he calls together his friends and neighbours, saying to them, 'Rejoice with me, for I have found my sheep which was lost!' I say to you that likewise there will be more joy in heaven over one sinner who repents than over ninety-nine just persons who need no repentance.'—Luke 15:6-8*

In Luke 10, Jesus sent his disciples out two by two to heal the sick and release the Kingdom of God in various cities.

> *'Then the seventy returned with joy, saying, 'Lord, even the demons are subject to us in Your name.' And He said to them, 'I saw Satan fall like lightning from heaven. Behold, I give you the authority to trample on serpents and scorpions, and over all the power of the enemy, and nothing shall by any means hurt you. Nevertheless, do not rejoice in this, that the spirits are subject to you, but rather rejoice because your names are written in heaven."—Luke 10:17-20*

When they came back, they were full of joy about the miraculous events they encountered. It amazed them that even the demons submitted to them. Jesus told them not to find joy in the authority He gave them, but rather, in the joy of their salvation, because their names are registered in heaven.

Now I have to say, it is utterly amazing when you see God's miraculous power at work when He heals the sick or sets people free through your prayers for them. It certainly brings a lot of joy. Yet, Jesus said our joy should be in our salvation, in the fact that our names are written in heaven ready to be ushered in when our times comes.

Elevation Worship have just written an incredible song about this. You can find *'My Testimony'* on YouTube. One stanza says it all:

> *'I believe in signs and wonders,*
> *I have resurrection power,*
> *Still the miracle that I just can't get over,*
> *My name is registered in heaven,*
> *My praise belongs to you forever.'*[23]

Living in the joy of salvation

Even when everything is going so bad that it's hard to find something to be joyful about, we find out ultimate joy is in our salvation. This is the joy of eternity and the joy of living in right and close relationship with God. If you do not yet know this joy of salvation or you aren't quite sure of where you stand with God and for eternity, then please know it is possible to have a joyous assurance of your acceptance by God and your future after death. It is simply a matter of accepting the free gift of salvation that Jesus offers (see the Selah section in Chapter 1).

The phrase 'the joy of my salvation' comes from Psalm 51. King David had committed adultery, got his mistress pregnant and then had her husband murdered. David did some pretty shocking things, and it's easy to think that it's sins such as these that God is speaking about, however the Bible tells us that *anything* that has missed the mark of holiness is sin. Not one of us is without sin (Romans 3:23). I believe we need to have a revelation of our sin in order to grasp the joy that comes from really understanding the salvation we have in Jesus Christ.

I remember a time about two years into our church plant. I had a deep time with God, and He convicted me of my pride, of not thinking I had much sin, which led me to not fully realising how much I needed Him. I knew I wasn't perfect, but I also felt like I was a victim (which I actually had been in some seasons of my life) and I used this to explain away my sin. That was one of those life-changing moments where I fully surrendered to God and confessed how much I needed His redemption. This ushered in a deeper sense of the joy of my salvation than I'd ever had before. As Jesus said in Luke 7, if we realise how much we have been forgiven and redeemed, then we will have greater capacity to obey the first commandment—to love the Lord our God with all our heart. We will also have a greater capacity to grasp the joy of our salvation at a deeper heart level.

> *'I tell you, her sins—and they are many—have been forgiven, so she has shown me much love. But a person who is forgiven little shows only little love.'—Luke 7:47 (NLT)*

In Psalm 51, David asked God to restore to Him the joy of salvation, to bring restoration to that joy that comes from the revelation of salvation. Sometimes we forget how amazing it is to have God's salvation! We forget that once we were lost in sin and far from God. We forget that because of God's great love for us He sent His son to pay the price of the death we should have had. We forget that the precious blood of Jesus was spilled on the cross so we can be close to God and live with Him forever. Next time you forget how amazing His grace is, ask Him to restore the joy of your salvation.

After asking God to wash and cleanse him, David asks God to 'make him' hear joy and gladness.

> *'Wash me, and I shall be whiter than snow. Make me hear joy and gladness ...'—Psalm 51:7-8*

There's a good prayer right there:

God: please make me hear joy and gladness. Don't let me hear condemnation and my past, make me hear the forgiveness I have in You. Don't let me hear guilt and shame but make me hear how you've saved me and given me right standing with You. Make me hear how amazing this is; make me 'recognise grace'.

King David had a habit of talking to his soul, which I believe is a helpful habit for us to develop to keep our joy. He told his soul to rejoice in the Lord. He made a declaration that his soul would be joyful in the Lord and in His salvation.

'And my soul shall be joyful in the LORD; it shall rejoice in His salvation.'—Psalm 35:9

Joy in fullness: spirit, soul, and body.

It is important to know we are made up of body (Greek word *soma*), soul (Greek word *psuché*) and spirit (Greek word *pneuma*).

'Now may the God of peace make you holy in every way and may your whole spirit and soul and body be kept blameless until our Lord Jesus Christ comes again.'—1 Thessalonians 5:23 (NLT)

Our physical body is self-explanatory. Our soul is who we are: our mind, will and emotions. Our spirit is the place where the Spirit of God comes and lives when we turn our lives over to Jesus and are baptised in the Holy Spirit.

When we are filled with the Holy Spirit—when we are in a place of surrender to God—we put our spirit in charge over our emotions and thoughts and will.

Derek Prince explains it well (emphasis added).

'In the original pattern of creation, the spirit of man came directly from God, related directly to God, and enjoyed a perfect ordered relationship with God ... Through the devastating effects of man's rebellion, however, his spirit was compromised, and his soul took over control. As a result, unregenerate man is now controlled by the three functions of his soul: the will, the intellect, and the emotions.

When God reconciles a person to Himself, His purpose is to restore the original order, by which He once again relates directly to the person's spirit, whose spirit in turn moves upon his soul, and the soul moves upon the body.

This explains the words of David in Psalm 103:1: **Bless the LORD, O my soul.** *Through faith, David's spirit had been reunited with God and was eager to worship Him. So,* **his spirit stirred up his**

> ***soul*** *to move upon his vocal organs to utter the appropriate words of worship. This is a good example of the original pattern of creation at work in David's life.*
>
> *So long as this pattern is in place, where our spirit remains in submission to God and our soul remains in submission to our spirit, we function in harmony with God and with ourselves. But if at any time we reassert our rebellion against God, our soul is no longer in submission to our spirit. The result? Our inner harmony is broken. All of us face this constant tension between the spirit and the soul.*[24]

So, when David says, 'My soul shall be joyful in the Lord', it is like he is instructing his soul to submit to what his spirit knows: the joy of salvation.

This is further shown in Hebrews, where we are instructed to use the Word of God, the Bible, like a sword that divides between our soul and spirit.

> *'For the Word that God speaks is alive and full of power [making it active, operative, energising, and effective]; it is sharper than any two-edged sword, penetrating to the dividing line of the breath of life (soul) and [the immortal] spirit, and of joints and marrow [of the deepest parts of our nature], exposing and sifting and analysing and judging the very thoughts and purposes of the heart.'—Hebrews 4:12 (AMPC)*

For the purposes of this book, the application here is when our soul is lacking in joy, so we take the sword (a passage from the Word of God) and speak it over ourselves. We declare God's Word to divide what is in our soul and make it submit to the Spirit of God.

We could liken it to when you cut the fat off a chicken thigh: you take a sharp knife and cut off the unhelpful part which is not good for you, so you are left with only the good part.

Reminding ourselves of the joy of salvation

Likewise, we see in Habakkuk, the example of reminding oneself to be joyful.

> 'Even though the fig trees have no blossoms, and there are no grapes on the vines; even though the olive crop fails, and the fields lie empty and barren; even though the flocks die in the fields, and the cattle barns are empty, yet I will rejoice in the Lord! I will be joyful in the God of my salvation!'—Habakkuk 3:17-18 (NLT)

You may like to do some further study on this passage. There is a great Bible study on YouVersion based around Habakkuk.[25]

Even though every circumstance in his life is abysmal, even though nothing is going to plan, despite all this, Habakkuk reminds himself and resolutely declares over himself: 'I *will be joyful in the God of my salvation!*'

It's almost like he is saying to himself:

> 'Self, you want to descend into self-pity and despair, but I will not let you. You will be joyful and that is what my will has decided so, my soul and thoughts and emotions, submit to that.'

He reminds his own self of the salvation he has in his God. He recalls that God and His salvation are enough to impart joy, no matter what else is going on.

I remember years ago in the worship time at church, there was a song about faith and joy. I thought to myself I am not going to sing this because I value integrity and being authentic and I did not feel I had much faith and joy in that moment. But then I heard God adjust my thinking. Like a still, small voice in my spirit, He instructed me that faith is not about feelings. He said, '*If you sing the song, it is not a lack of integrity; it is a matter of building your faith up.*' He reminded me of Jude 1:20-21 : 'But you, beloved, building yourselves up on your most holy faith, praying in the Holy Spirit, keep yourselves in the love of God, waiting for the mercy of our Lord Jesus Christ that leads to eternal life.' He then went on to say, *'As you sing, you will be declaring in faith, over your feelings, the truth of my Word and who I am. It is reminding yourself of the joy of your salvation and of knowing Me.'*

Jesus obviously knew we would easily forget the joy of our salvation and need to remind ourselves of his great sacrifice and free gift. To help us, he graciously invites us into communion, instructing us to break bread and drink wine together in remembrance of Him and to do it often.

> *'And when He had given thanks, He broke it and said, 'Take, eat; this is My body which is broken for you; do this in remembrance of Me.' In the same manner He also took the cup after supper, saying, 'This cup is the new covenant in My blood. This do, as often as you drink it, in remembrance of Me. For as often as you eat this bread and drink this cup, you proclaim the Lord's death till He comes."—1 Corinthians 11:24-26*

What a wonderful reminder we can take part in regularly to remember the absolute joy of the salvation we have because of Jesus' broken body and blood.

Selah: stop, connect, enjoy ...

This is a time to go to Jesus as our well of salvation.

Listen to the song Amazing Grace and ask Jesus to give you a revelation of how He has redeemed your life.

Remind yourself of the amazing grace given to you by God by taking communion and partaking in the bread and wine as Jesus instructs us, remembering His sacrifice. (1 Corinthians 11:24-26)

As you pray, ask God:

God, make me hear joy and gladness and restore the joy of my salvation.

God, show me how to use Your Word to divide my soul and spirit and understand your truth.

God, show me how to instruct my soul to submit to what my spirit knows.

Remind your self: I will be joyful ...

I will be joyful and that is what my will has decided so my soul and thoughts and emotions must submit to that.

Remind your self of the salvation you have in Christ Jesus, which is plenty to be joyful about, no matter what else is going on. (Habakkuk 3:17-18)

Ask Jesus to fill you with buckets of His living water. (John 4:13-14 and 7:37)

4. Joy is 'Considered'

The biblical Greek word for consider is '*hegesasthe*' and is a verb. It is something you make a considered choice about; a decision made from a conscious and informed position. The definition is: (a) To lead, (b) To think, be of opinion, suppose, consider.[26]

Interesting! So, it is a *doing* word. To apply this definition, the instruction is to lead myself into thinking and supposing and considering my trial as joy. It is like I need to lead myself into this choice, which supposes 'myself' doesn't automatically default to joy thus the instruction to lead myself there.

> '*Consider it nothing but joy, my brothers and sisters, whenever you fall into various trials. Be assured that the testing of your faith [through experience] produces endurance [leading to spiritual maturity, and inner peace]. And let endurance have its perfect result and do a thorough work, so that you may be perfect and completely developed [in your faith], lacking in nothing.*'—James 1:2-4 (AMP)

The English dictionary meaning of 'consider' is to think carefully about (something), typically before making a decision, think about and be drawn towards (a course of action), believe to be; think. A common phrase is 'all things considered'-taking everything into account.[27]

The Bible versions of ESV and NKJV sum it up well with the phrase, 'count it all joy'. When a trial comes along, we are to take everything into consideration and 'take account of ourselves'—our emotions, our thoughts, our responses, and our reactions—and credit it to our joy account.

Choosing the joy account

Joy is considered. It is not a feeling. It is not a reaction to something good. It is something you make a considered choice about; a decision made from a conscious and informed position.

We could credit our difficulties and trials to our self-pity account, our complaining account, our despair account, our glum account, our bitterness account, or our anxiety account. Instead, we are instructed to credit it to our *joy* account. Think back to what we learnt in Chapters 1 and 2 about what joy is and where it comes from. The key is to actually make the count, to consider and lead ourselves when it is all too easy to react without taking anything into account. We are asked to be proactive in realising that we have a choice to count and consider.

We are also called to 'gladden ourselves' and *decide* to rejoice in who the Lord is always, at all times, in good seasons and bad.

> *'Rejoice in the Lord always [delight, gladden yourselves in Him]; again, I say, Rejoice!'—Philippians 4:4 (AMPC)*

This means we need to choose to be glad-hearted, even when everything inside us wants to not rejoice. If He has asked us to do this, then He also provides the ability to do so—we have the ability to direct and rule our thinking and our attitudes. If we do, Proverbs tells us we will have a continual feast regardless of circumstances.

> *'All the days of the desponding and afflicted are made evil [by anxious thoughts and forebodings], but he who has a glad heart has a continual feast [regardless of circumstances].'—Proverbs 15:15 (AMPC)*

This is our promise if we are making that decision to have a glad heart. I see this as a feast inside our souls—a feast of wholeness, freedom, healing, joy, life, and peace.

God's ways and thoughts

Why would God instruct us to do something so counter-intuitive? Because His ways and thoughts are higher than ours and trump our ways and thoughts because He is the God of the entire universe and we are not. I am pleased this is the case! If God's ways and thoughts would fit into my limited understanding, then He wouldn't be God. I certainly would not feel as secure in serving and worshipping a God who was so finite and limited that He fit into my way of thinking.

> *'For My thoughts are not your thoughts, nor are your ways My ways,' says the Lord. 'For as the heavens are higher than the earth, so are My ways higher than your ways, And My thoughts than your thoughts.'—Isaiah 55:8-9*

It has been my experience over many years of searching out God's ways and thoughts, that when the benefit of hindsight becomes available, I can often look back and see His ways and thoughts are definitely higher than mine. Not always. Some things happen that will have to wait until the hindsight we will have in heaven. For now, we only know in part but then we will know in full.

> *'Now we see things imperfectly, like puzzling reflections in a mirror, but then we will see everything with perfect clarity. All that I know now is partial and incomplete, but then I will know everything completely, just as God now knows me completely.'—1 Corinthians 13:12 (NLT)*

Leading our inner selves

Proverbs calls us to have rule over, or have jurisdiction over, our own spirit. The consequence if we do not? We become like a broken city without walls, without boundaries.

> *'Whoever has no rule over his own spirit is like a city broken down, without walls.' Proverbs 25:28*

This speaks of ourselves leading our inner selves, instead of ourselves being reactionary to whatever comes our way, meaning we are responsible to set up our own boundaries.

I was looking for inspiration that explained further my point and came across this quote on Pinterest. As far as I know it's from Pastor Steven Furtick and it sums things up nicely:

> *'Your joy and peace are under your jurisdiction. No one can take them away without your permission.'*

Our sphere of influence, therefore, involves our own 'self' and guarding our joy and peace.

We have an amazing advantage over the writer of Proverbs which was written well before the birth of Jesus Christ. We live after Jesus came to earth, rose from the dead, returned to heaven, and left His Spirit to lead and empower us. We are not just asked to lead ourselves and rule over our spirit in our own strength but are empowered by the Holy Spirit to do this and to walk in step with Him.

If we connect this with James 1:2-4, we see the scripture gives us instruction in the light of trials being inevitable; whether or not we like it, it's a matter of *when* trials come our way, not if. And when they do, we are to stop and consider our reaction.

It's a chain reaction of the emotional kind

We all have natural reactions. These are default reactions that we fall back to when the pressure is on and will be different for everyone, but we all have them.

Psychologists say we have a stress response which causes us to either 'fight or flight or freeze'.[28] Some people are more likely to kick into fight mode. They can become overly busy, anxious, and striving, trying to work their way out of it. Some will rage and make life difficult for everyone around them. Some turn to addictive behaviour to have some sort of control over their life. Other people will 'flight'. They will retreat and hide away to pretend nothing is happening. They will isolate themselves from the world. Some will go into a 'freeze' mode where they are unable to do anything or numb the pain with addictions. Still others have more severe and detrimental reactions and harm themselves.

What is your default mode when a trial comes along? Mine is flight. I just want to hide away from everyone and everything and feel sorry for myself and become bitter. Some would say that this behaviour is indicative of needing some 'space' or rest, and whilst this is likely to be true, and we all need times of rest and space for our health and wellbeing, the response becomes unhealthy when we use it to withdraw because of pain.

I am also prone to numb my anxiety with a good movie/TV show to stop my thoughts, which of course then pop up in the middle of the night instead. Now there is nothing wrong with a good movie/TV show unless it is used excessively as an anaesthetic instead of processing something that should be processed. I must say I sometimes find it helpful to anaesthetise for a bit to let my thoughts rest awhile. But after the 'thoughts-rest', it's important to then face it. Dr Caroline Leaf, neuroscientist, explains a helpful way to do this.

How to sit with your uncomfortable feelings:

1. Observe them objectively by imagining you are looking at them as if in a museum
2. Note the emotions and write them down
3. Validate and accept them; don't punish yourself or judge the emotions
4. Focus on the present task at hand and set time aside later to do some more analysis on how you felt and the triggers[29]

Choosing a better way

Whether we have a fight-or-flight response, we all need to lead ourselves into the presence of God to process our pain.

We also need to lead ourselves to reach out for help if needed. Remember that sometimes we are not okay and that is okay. In those situations, I implore you to reach out for help. Reach out courageously and speak to someone who is wise and trustworthy.

We do well to lead ourselves into the place of peace that surpasses understanding by finding joy and strength in Jesus, the Prince of Peace.

I want to encourage you: have a practice next time a minor challenge comes your way. Instead of reacting in your usual, default manner, have a go at stopping and considering the opportunities involved.

Refer back to Dr Caroline Leaf's statement and ask God to show you how His joy can be a part of this difficulty if you process it in His Presence. If you start with a small trial, when a bigger trial comes, you will be better equipped to count it as joy.

Nick Vujicic, world renowned inspirational speaker who was born without arms or legs, proposes this: 'When faced with any difficulty, try to find the pure joy that's contained there.'[30]

Now let's make something clear. This doesn't mean that if there is a seriously bad circumstance we just pretend nothing is wrong, live in denial and try our best to be happy. As we discovered in Chapter 1, joy is not the same as being happy. God's joy can be present in even the worst of circumstances. I've experienced joy in some difficult times, but don't just take my word for it. Let's have a look at two amazing women who endured inconceivable trials and see what they have to say about joy.

Corrie ten Boom

During the Second World War, the Ten Boom home became a refuge, a hiding place, for fugitives and those hunted by the Nazis. By protecting these people, Casper, and his daughters, Corrie, and her sister Betsie, risked their lives. This non-violent resistance against the Nazi-oppressors was the Ten Booms' way of living out their Christian faith. This faith led them to hide Jews, students who refused to cooperate with the Nazis, and members of the Dutch underground resistance movement. On February 28, 1944, this family was betrayed by a fellow Dutch citizen and the Gestapo (Nazi secret police) raided their home.

Ten days after his arrest, their father Casper died in Scheveningen Prison. Betsie and Corrie also spent some time in that prison. From there, they were transported to camp Vucht and then to the notorious Ravensbrück Concentration Camp in Germany.

Life at Ravensbrück was almost unbearable, but Betsie and Corrie spent their time sharing Jesus' love with their fellow prisoners. Many women became Christians in that terrible place because of Betsie and

Corrie's witness to them. Betsie died at Ravensbrück (age 59), but Corrie miraculously survived.

After her release from Ravensbrück Concentration Camp (age 53) Corrie travelled all around the world to tell everyone that 'There is no pit so deep that God's love is not deeper still' and that 'God will give us the love to be able to forgive our enemies.' In more than 30 years, Corrie visited over 60 countries to testify to God's love and to encourage people with the message that 'Jesus is Victor.'[31] You can read her full story in her book *'The Hiding Place.'*

Corrie ten Boom was renowned for her understanding of the joy of the Lord, saying 'Joy runs deeper than despair,' and 'Happiness isn't something that depends on our surroundings … It's something we make inside ourselves.'[32]

If I imagine myself in Corrie's shoes, I think I may have had despair running deeper than joy. However, God is always ready to give grace and capacity to whatever He calls us to even in the most difficult of circumstances.

Elisabeth Elliot

Elisabeth attended Wheaton College and studied Greek because she wanted to translate the Bible for remote peoples of the world. While at Wheaton, she met Jim Elliot, and both went to Ecuador after graduation. They served in different parts of Ecuador the first year then married in Quito, Ecuador, in 1953 and later had a daughter, Valerie.

Jim felt a call to mission work among the unreached. This led him to the Aucas, a people that no outsider had encountered and survived. In 1955, Jim and four other men were speared to death when they attempted to make contact with the Aucas.

After Jim died, Elisabeth and her daughter Valerie, along with Rachel Saint—the sister of Nate Saint, one of the slain missionaries—lived among the Quichua tribe. Because of her tall height, the Aucas gave Elisabeth the tribal name *Gikari*, meaning 'Woodpecker.'

While living among the tribe, Elisabeth learned why Jim had been killed. The tribesmen were afraid that outsiders would come into their home and take away their freedom. With this new knowledge, Elisabeth said, 'The Auca was trying to preserve his own way of life, his own liberty. He believed the foreigners were a threat to that liberty, so he feels he had every right to kill them. In America, we decorate a man for defending his country.' Eventually, Elisabeth and Rachel were able to see many in the tribe come to faith in Christ.[33]

Elisabeth remarried but only four years later her new husband died of cancer. Here is a lady who is no stranger to trials. "She was a woman who remained faithful despite many trials and tribulations. Her faithfulness inspired and touched the lives of many around the world."[34]

Elisabeth Elliot's life work was to share these deepest things: the trustworthiness of God, the blessings of obedience, the hope of joy in the midst of sorrow, the call to love one's enemy, the priceless treasure of purity, and the true meaning of Biblical womanhood and manhood.[35]

She had a radio program for 13 years called 'Gateway to Joy' and had this to say about the subject—

"Everything, if given to God, can become your gateway to joy."[36]

Her 'everything' that became her 'gateway to joy' involved a lot of tragedy. We see from her example that it is truly possible to consider it all joy when trials come.

If we look at the stories of these two women who endured unimaginable pain and what they say about joy, it appears it is genuinely achievable to carry out God's instructions; to consider trials an opportunity for joy. (James 1:2-4)

Another great modern-day woman of God, Christine Caine, founder of A21[37] and speaker across the globe posted this on Instagram in the middle of the COVID-19 season.

'With much prayer, intentionality, and the Holy Spirit working in me during this season, I'm learning to choose joy—to turn simple and ordinary moments into extraordinary, joy-filled moments. I'm learning to view this season as an opportunity to see God at work with a whole new lens. To see joy, beauty, and goodness in ways I had never expected. To recover the joy I thought was lost. Our God is faithful. So faithful. He is willing to meet us in our deepest pain and be our true source of joy.' [38]

God is indeed willing to be our true source of joy. The question is: are we willing to consider joy in our trials?

Why consider trials as joy?

Why? Why are trials something to consider as joy? Sometimes it's easier to press into something if we know the reason. Let's look at the verse from James again, but this time in more detail. I've highlighted the extra words that really bring this scripture alive in the Amplified Bible, Classic Edition.

> *'Consider it **wholly joyful**, my brethren, whenever you are **enveloped in or encounter** trials **of any sort or fall into various temptations**. Be assured **and understand** that the trial and proving of your faith bring out endurance and **steadfastness and patience**. But let endurance **and steadfastness and patience have full play** and do a thorough work, so that you may be [people] perfectly and fully developed [with no defects], lacking in nothing.'—James 1:2-4 (AMPC)*

So, the 'why' is that our trial is testing our faith. This then produces endurance, spiritual maturity, and inner peace, bringing us into a place of having completely developed faith; faith that is not lacking, faith that has fortitude and resilience.

This next passage from Romans gives us further reason and shows us a crucial key; when we open up to the Holy Spirit and his guidance, he is able to pour the love of God into our hearts and fill us with joy!

> *'Moreover, [let us also be full of joy now!] let us exult and triumph in our troubles and rejoice in our sufferings, knowing that pressure and*

> *affliction and hardship produce patient and unswerving endurance. And endurance (fortitude) develops maturity of character (approved faith and tried integrity). And character [of this sort] produces [the habit of] joyful and confident hope of eternal salvation. Such hope never disappoints or deludes or shames us, for God's love has been poured out in our hearts through the Holy Spirit Who has been given to us.'—Romans 5:3-5 (AMPC)*

As we endure trials with joy, our character, faith, and hope grow into maturity. We transform from immature faith to mature faith; a faith that can overcome and withstand storms and provide the personal growth required to help others discover the peace of God that comforts us in all our troubles.

> *'He comforts us in all our troubles so that we can comfort others. When they are troubled, we will be able to give them the same comfort God has given us.'—2 Corinthians 1:4 (NLT)*

Furthermore, it brings us the joy and fulfilment of knowing that, with the empowerment of the Holy Spirit, we **can** endure and overcome.

> *'Yet in all these things we are more than conquerors and gain an overwhelming victory through Him who loved us [so much that He died for us]. For I am convinced [and continue to be convinced—beyond any doubt] that neither death, nor life, nor angels, nor principalities, nor things present and threatening, nor things to come, nor powers, nor height, nor depth, nor any other created thing, will be able to separate us from the [unlimited] love of God, which is in Christ Jesus our Lord.'—Romans 8:37-39 (AMP)*

Think of it like an athlete training for a marathon. I have a friend who would run ultra-marathons while raising five boys and having two jobs. I imagine she did not always enjoy getting up before the crack of dawn to train. Yet imagine the feeling of crossing the finish line! Crossing a marathon finish line will never be a reality for most of us, let alone an ultra-marathon; in fact, most of us would not even want it to be our reality, however, we have all pushed through some sort of endurance to reach a goal and see the reward. Long nights of study to obtain a good mark; denying our bodies to reach a fitness or weight goal; deciding to do the right thing when it is harder than the wrong thing; stepping out of fear to do something courageous. You can fill in your own _____

How?

Now I am quite a pragmatic person and I always like to look at the 'how'. It's all very well to have something as a theory, but how does it work in my everyday life? He says we are to be *doers* of the Word of God, not just hearers.

> *'But be doers of the word, and not hearers only, deceiving yourselves.'*
> —James 1:22

God calls us to put aside our default pattern and *decide* to consider trials as joy and has given us all the tools and instructions to be victorious in this so we can put aside our natural reactions to allow God to develop our faith. We *can* press in and welcome his work in our life through the trial. We can choose to live out the trial in His presence where there is fullness of joy. Let's review Psalms 16: 5-11 again.

> *Lord, you alone are my inheritance, my cup of blessing.*
> *You guard all that is mine.*
> *The land you have given me is a pleasant land.*
> *What a wonderful inheritance!*
> *I will bless the Lord who guides me;*
> *even at night my heart instructs me.*
> *I know the Lord is always with me.*
> *I will not be shaken, for he is right beside me.*
> *No wonder my heart is glad, and I rejoice.*
> *My body rests in safety.*
> *For you will not leave my soul among the dead*
> *Or allow your holy one to rot in the grave.*
> *You will show me the way of life,*
> *granting me the joy of your presence*
> *and the pleasures of living with you forever.*
> —Psalm 16:5-11 (NLT)

God has made us all so unique. That is so mind-blowing! Out of all the trillions of people that ever lived, we all have a different fingerprint! So the 'how' will be different for everyone but asking Holy Spirit to show us our 'how', is the key for each of us, regardless how we live out those instructions.

We meet for Bible study, prayer, and encouragement with some folks from church regularly and at the time of writing this book, because of COVID-19, we currently meet online to comply with the lockdown restrictions. As our city, Melbourne, went into the second round of lockdown, we asked each person how they are drawing on God through this time.

There are numerous ways to draw near to God through trials. Here are just a few ways that people are connecting with Him:

- spending time worshipping and praising God for who He is
- meditating and soaking in the Word of God and letting God's truth soak in
- painting, and God speaks and comforts while painting
- identifying thoughts that are deceptive and negative and renewing their mind with God's truth
- going for a walk and talking with God
- dancing or another creative expression
- journaling what God is saying personally and calling out to God for help
- resting in His Presence to receive His help and peace
- praying with a trusted friend and processing what God is saying to them by speaking it out loud in that safe space

Now what happens if the trial is because of Jesus; because we are living for Jesus? We see this throughout the New Testament and all through the world today. Many are losing their lives or being imprisoned even today, simply for trusting in Jesus. What does the Bible say about this? It says persecution can bring exceeding joy and that we can choose to rejoice.

I love my sons and I'm very proud of them for many reasons and asked their permission to share their high school stories. They were both teased for being a Christian and dealt with it in their own way. One was called 'The Christian Kid' as an insult. At first, it was very painful and affected him adversely, but not enough to stop sharing his faith. Over time, he decided to believe what Jesus said in Matthew 5:10 and declared himself as blessed because this was happening to him. The other son was called 'Super Religious Kid'. He came to a place of making a conscious decision that he would not allow it to get to him: with God's help, he chose joy. They both considered their trial as joy in their unique way.

> *'Blessed [comforted by inner peace and God's love] are those who are persecuted for doing that which is morally right, for theirs is the kingdom of heaven [both now and forever]. Blessed [morally courageous and spiritually alive with life-joy in God's goodness] are you when people insult you and persecute you, and falsely say all kinds of evil things against you because of [your association with] Me.'—Matthew 5:10-11 (AMP)*

Following are a few encouraging verses about finding joy in trials as a result of following Christ in case you think this is a misprint. It certainly does not make sense to our human way of thinking, but I can testify, as can countless others, that it is true. Remember, blessedness does not equal 'easy-ness', but deep joy.

> *'Beloved, do not think it strange concerning the fiery trial which is to try you, as though some strange thing happened to you; but rejoice to the extent that you partake of Christ's sufferings, that when His glory is revealed, you may also be glad with exceeding joy.'—1 Peter 4:12-13 (NKJV)*

The Greek joy word here in 1 Peter is chairete. This is what it means: 'favourably disposed, leaning towards' and cognate with xáris, 'grace')—properly, to delight in God's grace ('rejoice')—literally, to experience God's grace (favour), be conscious (glad) for His grace.[39]

As we saw in the first chapter, the meaning of joy in trials here is being conscious of, leaning towards and delighting in God's grace and favour towards us. Joy, in this instance, is considering what He did for us because of His great love. He gave His life on a horrendously cruel cross in our place. He then conquered all our sin, death, and pain by rising back to life through the exceeding greatness of His power (Ephesians 1:19-20). Now we have hope, forgiveness, freedom, and eternity!

Jesus promised us great joy when we are persecuted because we follow Him. We see throughout the New Testament the disciples of Jesus living this out and being filled with joy when they went through terrible trials of persecution. They carried on in the power of the Holy Spirit, bringing the love and good news and generosity of Jesus wherever they went.

> *'What blessings await you when people hate you and exclude you and mock you and curse you as evil because you follow the Son of Man. When that happens, be happy! Yes, leap for joy! For a great reward awaits you in heaven. And remember, their ancestors treated the ancient prophets that same way.'—Luke 6:22-24 (NLT)*

> *'And the word of the Lord was being spread throughout all the region. But the Jews stirred up the devout and prominent women and the chief men of the city, raised up persecution against Paul and Barnabas, and expelled them from their region. But they shook off the dust from their feet against them and came to Iconium. And the disciples were filled with joy and with the Holy Spirit.'—Acts 13:49-52 (NKJV)*

> *'Now I want you to know, dear brothers and sisters, what God in his kindness has done through the churches in Macedonia. They are being tested by many troubles, and they are very poor. But they are also filled with abundant joy, which has overflowed in rich generosity.'—2 Corinthians 8:1-2 (NLT)*

I'd like to finish this chapter with Paul's prayer for the church in Colossi, and my prayer for you.

'We also pray that you will be strengthened with all his glorious power so you will have all the endurance and patience you need. May you be filled with joy, always thanking the Father. He has enabled you to share in the inheritance that belongs to his people, who live in the light.'—Colossians 1:11-12 (NLT)

Selah: stop, connect, enjoy ...

It is time do some counting and considering.

Read this passage again and contemplate what it means for you in this season of your life.

> 'Consider it nothing but joy, my brothers and sisters, whenever you fall into various trials. Be assured that the testing of your faith [through experience] produces endurance [leading to spiritual maturity, and inner peace]. And let endurance have its perfect result and do a thorough work, so that you may be perfect and completely developed [in your faith], lacking in nothing.'—James 1:2-4 (AMP)

What is your default response, your natural reaction, when a trial comes?

We are all different. Ask the Holy Spirit to give you a unique tool that shows you how you can lead yourself into a place of considering and counting a trial as joy.

What stops you from leading yourself and ruling over your spirit? How can the Holy Spirit help you?

Take some time to ask the Holy Spirit to pour the love of God into your heart.

Meditate on the following passage and ponder how it can help you find joy on your life journey.

> 'We also pray that you will be strengthened with all his glorious power so you will have all the endurance and patience you need. May you be filled with joy, always thanking the Father. He has enabled you to share in the inheritance that belongs to his people, who live in the light.'—Colossians 1:11-12 (NLT)

5. Purpose Releases Joy

> *'We humans can tolerate suffering, but we cannot tolerate meaninglessness.'—Archbishop Desmond Tutu*

Not sure about you, but when I am feeling joy-less, I feel tired and flat. I feel like sleeping and letting go of all my good disciplines. I want to get that pity party started! I want to turn into a bit of a hermit and withdraw into myself. I feel like I need to be a bit pampered and if I go to God, I want Him to pamper me too and not ask anything too hard of me. Perhaps if I have some 'me-time' I will re-gain my joy.

So, you can imagine my surprise when, in my joy study, I found that finding joy is not linked to being pampered, but inherently linked to purpose.

God designs us to walk in the purpose He has created us for, and we find joy when we walk in those purposes.

> *'For we are His workmanship [His own masterwork, a work of art], created in Christ Jesus [reborn from above—spiritually transformed, renewed, ready to be used] for good works, which God prepared [for us] beforehand [taking paths which He set], so that we would walk in them [living the good life which He prearranged and made ready for us].'—Ephesians 2:10 (AMP)*

As a matter of fact, lack of purpose can cause us to lose our joy. For me, I thought it was the circumstances that caused me to lose my joy. Actually, my loss of joy was from letting go of my purpose *because* of the circumstances, and the resulting faulty mindsets I had taken on.

Purpose unlocks joy

In my journey to re-find joy, I was having a particularly 'low in joy' day and did not seem to be overcoming. I decided to pluck up the courage to ring a friend to ask her to pray for me. She prayed and sensed a word from God for me. She said, *'I'm not sure why, because it doesn't seem to relate to where you are at, but the word is:* **you were born for such** *a time as this*' (from Esther 4:14). As she spoke God's word to me, it went deep into my spirit and I felt a release of profound joy. If we think about it with our natural minds, it is surprising. It doesn't seem like the type of word to give someone when they need joy, but what it did was re-release purpose, which in turn, re-released joy. I was so glad I made that phone call.

If you are not getting any victory in getting your joy back and the enemy of our souls is trying all He can to steal it (John 10:10), then ask for help—always ask for help. It takes a lot of courage and usually when you are in the place where you need help, you feel more like isolating. But please press through the barrier and ask someone to pray for you and stand with you.

God made us to live in community, so always call someone if you are not overcoming on your own. This is such a powerful key to our growth and getting breakthroughs. Yes, we are to find our strength in the Lord and press into Him to find breakthrough, but He also made us to need each other. He calls us His people, His body, in which all parts are needed to interact with each other in order for the body to function well.

I would hope that all of us have someone we can talk things through with. If you don't, may I suggest you find someone as soon as possible? Someone you can discuss questions about life and faith with and can ask to pray for you if your joy is fading.

Let me share with you my findings about how joy is linked to purpose.

In the parable of the talents in Matthew 25, three people were given talents or gifts by their master who was off to do some extensive travel. One person was given five talents, one was given two, and the third was given one.

When the master asked what they had done with the talents upon his return, the five and two talent guys had doubled theirs. The one talent guy did nothing with his but hid it away so the master wouldn't get angry with what he'd done with it. Needless to say, the master was pretty upset with him.

> *'But his lord answered and said to him, 'You wicked and lazy servant, you knew that I reap where I have not sown and gather where I have not scattered seed. So, you ought to have deposited my money with the bankers, and at my coming I would have received back my own with interest. So, take the talent from him, and give it to him who has ten talents. 'For to everyone who has, more will be given, and he will have abundance; but from him who does not have, even what he has will be taken away. And cast the unprofitable servant into the outer darkness. There will be weeping and gnashing of teeth.'—Matthew 25:26-30*

The guy with the one talent thought he would do nothing because if he did something, he might get it wrong. But by doing nothing, he got it wrong. It was like the master was saying to him: 'you could have at least done something, anything with it. Even if not the highest purpose of multiplying it, at least you could have invested it.' Doing nothing with it brought him no joy, only darkness and weeping.

Contrast this with the reply to the two who had used their talents and doubled them.

> *'His lord said to him, 'Well done, good and faithful servant; you were faithful over a few things, I will make you ruler over many things. Enter into the joy of your lord.'"—Matthew 25:21*

By using their gifts and talents, they were able to enter into the joy of the Lord. It didn't matter how many talents they had. One had more than the other. Both received the same commendation and joy reward.

The two-talent guy could have easily been distracted from using the two talents by looking at the five-talent guy and entering into comparison. This would have prevented the reward of entering into joy. We can see from this that comparison zaps joy (more about that in Chapter 8). Instead, he used his talents and doubled them and was rewarded with being granted the joy of his master.

Finding your sweet spot

Max Lucado speaks of finding your 'sweet spot', your place of purpose.

> 'Ever swung a baseball bat or paddled a Ping-Pong ball? If so, you know the oh-so-nice feel of the sweet spot. Life in the sweet spot rolls like the downhill side of a downwind bike ride. But you don't have to swing a bat or a club to know this. What engineers give sports equipment, God gave you. A zone, a region, a life precinct in which you were made to dwell. He tailored the curves of your life to fit an empty space in his jigsaw puzzle. And life makes sweet sense when you find your spot.'—Max Lucado[40]

The sweet spot is when you are walking in your purpose. Think of those times when you feel like you are flying. When it feels like this is what you were made to do. When what you are doing energises you instead of depleting you. It is here, in your sweet spot, where joy and fulfilment are found.

Some people find their sweet spot early in life, for others it may take years. The sweet spot is where everything intersects—your strengths, your spiritual gifts, your talents, your everyday life, what you enjoy, what energises you and God's calling and purpose for you. For some, they can even make a living out of their sweet spot and that is the ideal, but often not the real.

Living from the sweet spot positions you to enter into joy. As did the wise ones in the parable of the talents, be intentional about discovering and using your talents and gifts to position yourself to enter into the joy of the Lord.

Scientific research published in the US National Library of Medicine in 2013 confirmed a link between emotional health and purpose in life.

> 'Having purpose in life may motivate reframing stressful situations to deal with them more productively, thereby facilitating recovery from stress and trauma ... Purpose in life predicts both health and longevity suggesting that the ability to find meaning from life's

experiences, especially when confronting life's challenges, may be a mechanism underlying resilience.[41]

It is quite an interesting read if you'd like to delve into this scientific paper. The findings show that to respond well and recover from trauma and negative circumstances, it is helpful to have a purpose in life.

The paper also found purpose may underpin resilience, which is 'the ability to adapt successfully in the face of stress and adversity.'[42] Resilience is certainly something to cultivate in our lives, so when 'stuff happens', we can adapt and keep our joy.

Jesus: Our Mentor—finding joy through purpose

Let's have a look at Jesus, our ultimate example, who found joy in His purpose.

> *'... focusing our eyes on Jesus, who is the Author and Perfector of faith [the first incentive for our belief and the One who brings our faith to maturity], who for the joy [of accomplishing the goal] set before Him endured the cross, disregarding the shame, and sat down at the right hand of the throne of God [revealing His deity, His authority, and the completion of His work].'—Hebrews 12:2 (AMP)*

It seems offensive to have the word joy in the same sentence as the words 'endured the cross'. The Roman cross was no picnic. It's not very pleasant to read the details, but it displaces our sanitised view of Jesus on the cross we see in art.

> *'The accused needed to be nailed to the patibulum while lying down, so Jesus is thrown to the ground, reopening His wounds, grinding in dirt, and causing bleeding. They nail His 'hands' to the patibulum. The Greek meaning of 'hands' includes the wrist. It is more likely that the nails went through Jesus' wrists ... If placed in the wrist, the bones in the lower portion of the hand support the weight of the arms and the body remains nailed to the cross. The huge nail (seven to nine inches long) damages or severs the major nerve to the hand (the median nerve) upon impact. This causes continuous agonizing pain up both of Jesus' arms*

> ... It is highly likely that Jesus' feet were nailed through the tops as often pictured. In this position, the weight of the body pushes down on the nails and the ankles support the weight ... Again, the nail would cause severe nerve damage (it severs the dorsal pedal artery of the foot) and acute pain.
>
> Normally, to breathe in, the diaphragm (the large muscle that separates the chest cavity from the abdominal cavity) must move down. This enlarges the chest cavity and air automatically moves into the lungs (inhalation). To exhale, the diaphragm rises up, which compresses the air in the lungs and forces the air out (exhalation). As Jesus hangs on the cross, the weight of His body pulls down on the diaphragm and the air moves into His lungs and remains there. Jesus must push up on His nailed feet (causing more pain) to exhale.
>
> In order to speak, air must pass over the vocal cords during exhalation. The Gospels note that Jesus spoke seven times from the cross. It is amazing that despite His pain, He pushes up to say 'Forgive them' (Luke 23:34).
>
> The difficulty surrounding exhalation leads to a slow form of suffocation. Carbon dioxide builds up in the blood, resulting in a high level of carbonic acid in the blood. The body responds instinctively, triggering the desire to breathe. At the same time, the heart beats faster to circulate available oxygen. The decreased oxygen (due to the difficulty in exhaling) causes damage to the tissues and the capillaries begin leaking watery fluid from the blood into the tissues. This results in a build-up of fluid around the heart (pericardial effusion) and lungs (pleural effusion). The collapsing lungs, failing heart, dehydration, and the inability to get sufficient oxygen to the tissues essentially suffocate the victim. The decreased oxygen also damages the heart itself (myocardial infarction) which leads to cardiac arrest. In severe cases of cardiac stress, the heart can even burst, a process known as cardiac rupture. Jesus most likely died of a heart attack. [43]

This is what Jesus endured for the joy set before Him. And this biological description does not consider the spiritual and emotional pain He endured. Spiritually, Jesus carried the weight of the sins of the whole world and all who have ever lived. That's an unfathomable amount of guilt and weight to bear.

> *'But he was pierced for our rebellion, crushed for our sins. He was beaten so we could be whole. He was whipped so we could be healed. All of us, like sheep, have strayed away. We have left God's paths to follow our own. Yet the Lord laid on him the sins of us all.'*—Isaiah 53:5-6 (NLT)

> *'He personally carried our sins in His body on the cross [willingly offering Himself on it, as on an altar of sacrifice], so that we might die to sin [becoming immune from the penalty and power of sin] and live for righteousness; for by His wounds you [who believe] have been healed.'*—1 Peter 2:24 (AMP).

Jesus' purpose was to be sent from heaven to release the Kingdom of God on earth and pay the punishment for the sin of all humankind. His purpose was to come to earth to love and redeem humanity and pay the punishment of sin on the cross that was rightly ours to pay. And because He was in His Father's will fulfilling His purpose, He could see joy ahead.

God sent Jesus, His son, because He loved us so much that He didn't wish for any to perish but to have everlasting life. And I am beyond grateful that Jesus said yes. Jesus cried out through His pain in the garden of Gethsemane: 'Please Father take this cup from me, but nevertheless, not my will but yours.' (Matthew 26:39).

This was the joy set before Him. His vision and mission and purpose: to see His beloved people, you, and I, reconciled back into a loving relationship with God, as sons and daughters coming into glory.

> *'God, for whom and through whom everything was made, chose to bring many children into glory. And it was only right that he should make Jesus, through his suffering, a perfect leader, fit to bring them into their salvation.'*—Hebrews 2:10 (NLT)

The Passion paraphrase says this about the joy set before Jesus:

> *'Because his heart was focused on the joy of knowing that you woulbe his, he endured the agony of the cross and conquered its humiliation, and now sits exalted at the right hand of the throne of God!'*— Hebrews 12:2 (TPT)

Here we see Jesus considering joy at His worst hour on the cross because He was right in the middle of His purpose and because of His great love for us.

Now if we take our joy definitions from Chapter 1 and apply them to purpose, what do we find?

Joy is grace recognised. Grace is the empowering Presence of God enabling you to be who He created you to be, and to do what He has called you to do. When applied to purpose, if we live with a grateful recognition of His grace and allow His presence to empower us in our purpose, we find the place of joy. We find the place where we are invited to enter into the joy of our Lord.

Allow me to give you a personal example from this season. As I mentioned earlier, at the time of writing this book we are in the middle of a global pandemic. We live in Melbourne, Australia, and we had Lockdown 1.0 then had some restrictions eased. The cases then increased dramatically, so we went into Lockdown 2.0 with very stringent restrictions. We had compulsory masks, 8.00pm curfew, travel limited to 5km radius from our home, one-hour limit for exercise and no visitors.

In Lockdown 1.0, I saw it as a bit of a rest from being busy. I picked up writing this book again (after my short season of writers block I mentioned earlier) and wrote now and then. As we entered Lockdown 2.0, I decided to be more disciplined with my time and not waste God's precious time He has given me on this earth.

My routine changed to suit my intentions: a few days every week, I got up early and had my time with God (I even changed the way I do this according to how I felt God instructing me). I spent time worshipping Him in His Presence and praying before I did my Bible study. I then did some work on this book and then some exercise before I started work (from home) at 8.30am.

Getting up this early, in my mind, should have made me weary. However, it had the exact opposite effect. I found myself to be so much more joyful in Lockdown 2.0 than 1.0, and it came from spending time in the presence of God as my first priority. This set my day up very nicely and gave me a routine during a very unpredictable season. Incidentally, medical experts contend that routine is helpful for our mental health. Without routine, we can adopt unhealthy coping mechanisms and have decision fatigue,[43] which is a pretty bad thing to have during a season of unknown outcomes.

This joy also comes from purpose. I was given a prophetic word over 25 years ago that I would write a book and again from a close friend of ours a few times over the years. During this second lockdown, I was praying and felt an urgency to write and to finish this book as soon as possible. I absolutely loved it. Why? Because I believed it was my purpose for this season. Even if my story and research help just one person re-find their joy, it is definitely my purpose for this season.

I can understand that the concept of joy being born from purpose could be problematic. If you don't yet know what your talents and purpose are, how could you even get close to finding joy, right?

I have three things for you to consider about this mysterious connection:

1. We are created to live in community and give
2. Purpose is found in the everyday aspects of lives
3. Finding purpose comes from being intentional

1. We are created for community

The first thing to remember is we are created to live in community and be givers. Elisabeth Elliot (we saw her story in Chapter 4) says this about finding joy:

> *'The world looks for happiness through self-assertion. The Christian knows that joy is found in self-abandonment. 'If a man will let himself be lost for My sake,' Jesus said, 'he will find his true self.'*[44]

We can be sure that whatever our purpose is, it will be to bless others, not to focus on ourselves. Whatever talents we have been given are for building: to build up other people and to build God's Kingdom. Yes, also to build ourselves up in our faith, but to what end? So, we don't cause division (tearing down as opposed to building up) and to keep ourselves in the love of God.

> *'These are sensual persons, who cause divisions, not having the Spirit. But you, beloved, building yourselves up on your most holy faith, praying in the Holy Spirit, keep yourselves in the love of God, looking for the mercy of our Lord Jesus Christ unto eternal life.'*—Jude 1:19-21

Our purpose can be quite simple in terms of making a difference; it doesn't have to be to change the whole world (although it may be). If you have a talent for cooking, cook a meal for someone in need. If you're a skilled listener, take some time to lend an ear because this is rare in our modern, fast-paced world. If you can build or fix things, help a friend or neighbour in need with something in their house that needs doing. If you have a talent for hearing God and seeing in the Spirit, ask God who needs a word from Him today and give it to them. If you are an encourager, reach out and encourage someone, and if you have a talent for giving or serving, find someone who needs a financial blessing or needs practical help.

> *'In his grace, God has given us different gifts for doing certain things well. So, if God has given you the ability to prophesy, speak out with as much faith as God has given you. If your gift is serving others, serve them well. If you are a teacher, teach well. If your gift is to encourage others, be encouraging. If it is giving, give generously. If God has given you leadership ability, take the responsibility seriously. And if you have a gift for showing kindness to others, do it gladly.'*—Romans 12:6-8 (NLT)

2. Purpose is found in the everyday journey of life

The second point is that purpose is found in the everyday and it is a journey.

Sometimes we think we need to find our big major purpose for our lives, and we need to know it *now*. We can fall into the trap of thinking that if we don't have some big plan and don't know our main purpose for our entire lives, then we don't know our purpose. Even if we do know our major purpose, it is still a day by day intention of stepping into it.

We can start with what we do know. It's like a journey up the mountain of life. One step in front of the other and if we keep going in an upward direction, we will reach the top. Although sometimes there are some downwards moments too and we shouldn't be either surprised or discouraged by those times; it's just life. As singer Robert Breault says, of the optimist, 'someone who figures that taking a step backward after a step forward is not a disaster, it's more like a cha-cha.'[45]

There are so many examples of people failing at first and then finding their purpose was different to what they thought. For example, George Clooney thought his purpose was baseball. Gerard Butler studied law but was fired from his first job. Abraham Lincoln tried a military career where he got demoted from captain to private.

So, the point is to give something a go; see if it is your talent and gift or not. And, if you ask God for direction and guidance, then you're already way ahead since He made you and knows what He made you for. If you get up every day and ask God what your purpose is for that day and walk in that, then your journey will take you in the right direction up to the summit of that mountain called life.

3. Finding purpose comes from being intentional

The third point is to be intentional about finding purpose and walking in it.

If you don't know what talents you have been created with, there is a great tool called SHAPE in Rick Warren's book *The Purpose Driven Life*[46] if you need some help. And, as I mentioned in point one, we are made to be in community, so ask others around you—the wise others—what do you think my talents and gifts are? What do you see in me?

In this journey, may I suggest you take some time with God regularly to ask Him what your purpose in life is for this current season? We each go through different seasons and there will quite likely be a different purpose for each one. I like to start each year with a day seeking God. I call it my spiritual stocktake. I go somewhere beautiful, preferably near a beach, and have a blank page and ask God to write His purposes for me for the year ahead. It doesn't have to be the start of the year; it can be the start of a life season.

In conclusion, when you feel joy-less, rather than give in to the temptation to sleep it off or dull it out, try pressing in to finding purpose. If you are struggling, ask for help and input. Find your 'sweet spot', use your talents, and enter into the joy of your Lord.

Selah: stop, connect, enjoy …

Take some time with God to ask Him what your purpose is; what your 'sweet spot' is.

> *'For we are God's masterpiece. He has created us anew in Christ Jesus, so we can do the good things he planned for us long ago.'*—Ephesians 2:10 (NLT)

Ask Father God, what was I born for?

When you created me as your masterpiece, what are the good things you had planned for me in this season? What are the good things you had planned for me for today, for this week?

Have a look at the article listed in the endnotes about SHAPE[47]—or even read the whole 'The Purpose Driven Life'[48] book.

Think of someone who is wise, who knows you well and who you trust. Ask them—what do you see in me? What are my talents and gifts? What is my purpose in this season?

As I mentioned previously, I thought it was the circumstances that caused me to lose my joy. Actually, my loss of joy was from letting go of my purpose because of the circumstances, and the resulting faulty mindsets I had taken on.'

Ask yourself: are there faulty mindsets I have taken on because of my circumstances?

Ask yourself this question: have I let go of some of my purpose in life because I've let my circumstances drag me down?

6. Gratitude Releases Joy

> *'Gratitude produces deep, abiding joy because we know that God is working in us, even through difficulties.'*—Dr Charles Stanley

On my journey to re-find joy, I have concluded that joy is found when we have an 'attitude of gratitude'.

During the season when I had my 'joy crisis' a few years back, my husband Paul initiated a '10-day thankfulness challenge' on Facebook. The concept was to wake up and thank God for ten things for ten days. It has to be ten different, specific things, not the same and not generalised.

It changed everything for me!

Here's why: forming this habit transformed my thinking; it transformed me by the renewing of my mind, and it can do the same for anyone who makes the decision to be transformed.

Be counterculture

The 'behaviour and customs of this world' are to always want more and never be content with what you have; to look for the problem instead of looking for an opportunity for thankfulness. But God has a different, countercultural point of view:

> *'Don't copy the behaviour and customs of this world, but let God transform you into a new person by changing the way you think. Then you will learn to know God's will for you, which is good and pleasing and perfect.'*—Romans 12:2 (NLT)

Notice how this passage also links us back into our last chapter; into purpose? When we change the way we think, we will know God's perfect and pleasing will for us. In fact, giving thanks and being joyful is actually His will for us!

'Always be joyful. Never stop praying. Be thankful in all circumstances, for this is God's will for you who belong to Christ Jesus.'—1 Thessalonians 5:16-18 (NLT)

A question I hear over and over is: what is the will of God for my life?

The answer is simple: the will of God is to 'always be joyful'; to 'never stop praying' and 'be thankful in all circumstances.'

If you want to know God's will for your life, those three directives are your starting point.

1. Be joyful always
2. Make your life a prayer
3. Be thankful during every circumstance

From this place of intentionally following God's will in these internal attitudes of gratitude, prayer and joy, you will find the external areas of your life will line up to His as a result. Your ears will be open to hear God leading where to step and where not to step. Your heart will be open to walk in step with the Holy Spirit and walk into the open doors God opens and not through the doors He shuts.

Could following His plan each day in this way be the answer to finding God's will for our lives in the larger questions of life? If every day we are thankful to God and pray and choose His joy, then every day, with each step, He will lead us along His paths and purposes for our life.

Allow me to suggest that if life is getting you down, if circumstances are making you 'glum', make a list of what you can be thankful for. Start by making a conscience decision; make it your quest, your pursuit to turn the attitude of your heart from 'want and need' to gratitude. Ask 'What can I give thanks for?' in place of grumbling and see what happens!

Flip introspective grumpiness into meditative gratitude

Flip and smile! Yes, smile. There are actually scientifically proven reasons why we should smile—who knew!

> *'Each time you smile, you throw a little feel-good party in your brain. The act of smiling activates neural messaging that benefits your health and happiness ... For starters, smiling activates the release of neuropeptides that work toward fighting off stress (3). Neuropeptides are tiny molecules that allow neurons to communicate. They facilitate messaging to the whole body when we are happy, sad, angry, depressed, or excited. The feel-good neurotransmitters—dopamine, endorphins and serotonin—are all released when a smile flashes across your face as well. This not only relaxes your body, but it can also lower your heart rate and blood pressure ... The endorphins also act as a natural pain reliever—100-percent organic and without the potential negative side effects of synthetic concoctions ... Finally, the serotonin release brought on by your smile serves as an anti-depressant/mood lifter.'*[49]

In my quest to re-find joy, I found a list of the benefits of smiling. I can't find the exact list again, but there are many variations with similar points.

- Smiling is contagious.
- Smiling lowers stress and anxiety.
- Smiling releases endorphins and serotonin.
- You'll be more attractive.
- Smiling strengthens your immune system.
- You'll be more approachable.
- You'll seem more trustworthy.
- Smiling actually retrains your brain for the better.
- Smiling boosts your productivity.
- Smiling makes you more creative.
- Smiles are free!

So, I did a little experiment. I thought to myself; 'right, I am going to try smiling as the first thing I do when I wake up in the morning. Let's see if that helps with my lack of joy'.

My husband is a morning person, and he wakes up naturally this way; all bright and excited about the day! Since I had babies and 'had' to be a morning person, I actually enjoy being a morning person, but it doesn't come naturally.

Some people wake up and say, *'Good morning, Lord.'* Others say, *'Good Lord, it's morning.'* Which one are you?—*Unknown*

When the alarm goes off, my natural response is *'aaarrggh it's morning, I don't want to get out of bed!'*.

But I persevered, so no surprises after reading the scientific evidence of smiling, that my little experiment did make a significant difference. In addition, when combined with an attitude of gratitude, the difference between the days I smiled and was thankful and the days when I didn't were like night and day; dark and light; grey and multi-coloured.

Try it! Have a smile right now-release those endorphins and serotonin. Strengthen your immune system. Stimulate that creativity.

Why don't you try waking up and smiling before you even move in the morning and thank the Lord for His blessings in your life? Then wake up and smile with thankfulness every morning after that and see what happens.

As the wisdom of Proverbs advises, let your mouth bring you joy by your answer to your alarm clock and your answer to your thoughts throughout the day.

> *'A man has joy by the answer of his mouth, and a word spoken in due season, how good it is!'*—*Proverbs 15:23*

Time to get generous!

A close cousin of gratitude is generosity. If we are thankful for what we have, we are ready to give of ourselves, our time, our money, and our lives. If we are thankful for what we have, we can look at others, see what they have, and not feel like we are missing out. We can look at others and see the possibility of what we can give; how we can be excited when good things happen to those around us and how can we bless them.

The apostle Paul tells us that the church in Macedonia were in such a dreadful place of 'severe difficulty and tremendous suffering', yet they were filled with joy. How? They had an attitude of generosity. They gave beyond themselves; beyond their means; they were beyond generous.

> '...we want to tell you about the grace of God which has been evident in the churches of Macedonia [awakening in them a longing to contribute]; for during an ordeal of severe distress, their abundant joy and their deep poverty [together] overflowed in the wealth of their lavish generosity. For I testify that according to their ability, and beyond their ability, they gave voluntarily, begging us insistently for the privilege of participating in the service for [the support of] the saints.'—2 Corinthians 8:1-4 (AMP)

Joy does not come from clenching on to what we have, being discontent and always wanting more, or from an attitude of envy and stinginess. Joy comes from giving of ourselves, not just financially but also in time and kindness. Joy comes from being content and thankful, and from an attitude of gratitude and generosity.

Perspective bolsters gratitude

Another close relative of gratitude is perspective.

> 'Perhaps nothing helps us make the movement from our little selves to a larger world than remembering God in gratitude. Such a perspective puts God in view in all of life, not just in the moments we set aside for worship or spiritual disciplines. Not just in the moments when life seems easy.'[50]

If we view life by 'recognising God's grace' through a lens of gratitude, our perspective shifts and makes way for joy. When we view life through what God says in His Word, the way we see things, and what we focus on shifts from the transient to the eternal.

You've probably heard the perspective quote: 'It doesn't matter if the glass if half empty or half full ... Be grateful that you have a glass, and there is something in it ... '—Unknown

I recently saw a photo on Facebook of a dog. I seriously could not see anything other than a dog! Apparently, some people saw a creepy clown. Even when it was pointed out to me, I could only see a dog. *Perspective.*

You may have seen a YouTube video called 'First World Problems.'[51] It's a satirical look at how ridiculous it sounds when we express our small grievances compared with the issues of the third world nations. It's very amusing and gives us a tongue-in-cheek reminder to keep the little things in perspective, especially when the narrator mentions starving children in third world countries.

So, I will never forget my perspective being challenged along those lines a few years back when I received a letter from our sponsor boy in Uganda. He had been rescued from being a child soldier and, as he answered questions about his life, he asked for prayer that the men who are currently taking boys to become soldiers would not take him this time! At the end of his letter, there was a space where he could write anything he liked to us. Out of anything he could have chosen to write, he wrote: 'I am praying for you that God would bless you'.

I think I cried for an hour! Here was a young boy in Africa—who could be taken at any time as a child solider—praying for us in our blessed, Australian life. It certainly turned my perspective to gratitude for my life.

As we saw earlier in Romans 12:2, we are to 'be transformed by the renewing of your mind.' Part of renewing our mind is not thinking the way the world thinks but changing our perspective to the way God thinks.

God's perspective is a high and all-encompassing perspective. The Bible tells us God is all powerful, all wise and all knowing. He knows the end from the beginning. He knows all things.

From what perspective are we seeing life? Situations? Circumstances? Emotions? Problems? Expectations? Misunderstandings? And even positive times?

We can either see from our own perspective, from the devil's perspective, from the perspective of friends and family, from the world's perspective or, we can see from God's perspective; from a Kingdom perspective.

> *It is helpful to ask ourselves this question—from what perspective am I seeing this?*

Have you heard the expression: 'seeing from a bird's-eye view'? Birds can see remarkably long distances and with great accuracy. If their eyesight is bad, however, they become undernourished because they can't find food. If we are to see God's food for our souls and be nourished with His joy in all circumstances, we need that bird's-eye view from heaven's perspective.

The dictionary meaning of perspective is 'a way of regarding situations, facts, etc., and judging their relative importance; a mental view or outlook.'[52] So how do we judge the relative importance of situations in our lives?

> *'We do not look at the things which are seen, but at the things which are not seen. For the things which are seen are temporary, but the things which are not seen are eternal.'*—2 Corinthians 4:18

> *'Now faith is the substance of things hoped for, the evidence of things not seen.'*—Hebrews 11:1

What are you fixing our eyes on? Are you seeing the seen or the unseen? Of course, it's much easier to see the seen, but faith calls us to see the unseen.

Let's look at some of the options we choose to see from.

Our own perspective. We can look through the lens of:
- what's always been
- how it makes me feel
- what's best for me
- my value and belief systems shaped by experiences and background
- my fears—the fear lens is an irrational, distorted lens
- my sin and pride; I don't want to see it differently; I'd have to change
- inflexible attitudes about growing in Jesus: 'that's just me, I'm just like that'

From the devil's perspective. He is the father of lies, the accuser of the brethren, accusing us day and night using:
- condemnation (different to conviction); things can't change now you've done such bad things; you've dug yourself into a hole you can't get out of
- shame; it's all your fault for being so wrong
- spirit of fear, intimidation, rejection, etc. (If this is the case we need others to pray it off).
- words of our family and friends that he twists so that we feel attacked even when those words were not delivered with that intention

From the perspective of friends and family:
- parents; we need to honour them but see what they say from God's perspective
- peers and the pressure to conform
- seeking approval of others; what will they think of me?

From society's perspective:
- the patterns of this world which are so opposite to Kingdom patterns
- social media commentary
- fake news spread to cause confusion, dissention, fear
- pressure to conform to society's norms
- pressure to normalise unchristian behaviours such as swearing, gossiping, judging.

We have free will to choose from any of these points of perspective, but the best option is to see (to know and understand things) from God's perspective, from the King's perspective.

> '... that the God of our Lord Jesus Christ, the Father of glory, may give to you the spirit of wisdom and revelation in the knowledge of Him, the eyes of your understanding being enlightened; that you may know what is the hope of His calling, what are the riches of the glory of His inheritance in the saints ... '—Ephesians 1:17-18

'Objects in the mirror are closer than they appear'

Artists will tell you that objects that are closer seem bigger. So if you want an object to appear closer, you make it bigger. Consequently, something further away may be actually bigger, but it seems smaller. It's the same in life. Our circumstances are closer to us, so they seem bigger. God sees all the way from heaven. He has the long distance, big picture perspective of our lives. He may sometimes seem smaller to us or distant, but He's actually so big that He's bigger than our understanding can ever grasp. The extraordinary dichotomy is that God is bigger than we can imagine, but He is also close and personal, and He knows and cares about every intimate detail of our life.

> 'When I look at the night sky and see the work of your fingers—the moon and the stars you set in place—what are mere mortals that you should think about them, human beings that you should care for them?'—Psalm 8:3-4

It's a deliberate decision to shift our focus. It must be a deliberate choice, or we'll fix our eyes on what's easier. When I used to play squash with my Dad, when I was a little girl, he would pretend to pull out his eye and put it on the squash ball and told me to keep my eye on the ball. He did this every time, and though it was annoying, it was highly effective.

We need to get our eyes and fix them on God's 'ball' so we don't miss what He sees, how He views the situation and what His will is regarding it.

Here is a prayer from my heart to yours which summaries a lot of what I've written:

> '... ask that you may be filled with the knowledge of His will in all wisdom and spiritual understanding; that you may walk worthy of the Lord, fully pleasing Him, being fruitful in every good work and increasing in the knowledge of God; strengthened with all might, according to His glorious power, for all patience and longsuffering with joy; giving thanks to the Father who has qualified us to be partakers of the inheritance of the saints in the light.'—Colossians 1:9-11

Chicken or egg?

It's a bit like the chicken and the egg in this passage. What comes first? Does joy come first and giving thanks flows out of that? Or does joy with longsuffering come because of the thanksgiving and being strengthened with all might? Either way, it's all linked.

We are filled with spiritual understanding, so we have 'grace recognised' which gives us a desire to walk worthy of God and please Him in the purposes He has for us. We give thanks to Him and we receive empowerment and strength to suffer-long and have joy in the midst of it, which makes us thankful.

It's a cycle. If we want to break the cycle of 'no-joy', we can go to our source and ask Him to fill us and thank Him. We can resolve to recognise His amazing grace and thank Him. We can consider our life pure joy no matter the circumstance and bear fruit in His purpose for us and thank Him. We can think on and recognise how He has taken us out of darkness into light, which makes us thank Him more and recognise His grace, which in turn produces joy.

> 'It is only with gratitude that life becomes rich!'—Dietrich Bonhoeffer

We all wish for a rich life, a rich internal life, a life of joy. Start with gratitude. Make it your aim to be thankful, to start the day with thankfulness. Flip your attitude to one of gratitude and don't forget to smile.

Selah: stop, connect, enjoy ...

It's time to check our 'gratitude' thermometer.

> *'Always be joyful. Never stop praying. Be thankful in all circumstances, for this is God's will for you who belong to Christ Jesus.'—1 Thessalonians 5:16-18 (NLT)*

Write a list of practical ways you can follow God's will for you in the three ways outlined in this Scripture.

1. I can be joyful by:
2. I can pray continually by:
3. I can be thankful by:

Be honest and ask yourself: Have I got an attitude of gratitude? Or have I got some other unhelpful attitude and what is it?

Ask God in what ways can you be generous. It could be generous with time, finances, encouragement, mercy, etc. Ask Him if there are any perspective shifts he would like to point out to you.

Practice breaking this cycle right now:

> *Lord God, I ask you to fill me. I thank you for filling me with your amazing grace. I declare that my life is one of pure joy no matter my circumstances. Please reveal to me your purpose for my life so I can bear fruit for your purposes. Help me to recognise your grace, that you have taken me from darkness to light and set me free and given me joy in return. Amen.*

Take a 'smile challenge'. Every morning for the next three weeks, wake up and smile before you do anything else, before you even move.

Take a '10-day thankfulness challenge'. Every morning for the next 10 days, thank God for 10 different, specific things. Then let it extend from 10 days to the rest of your life.

7. JOY Busters: Worry, Fear, Shame & Guilt

Remember the old movie Ghostbusters? The song went like this:

*'If there's something strange in your neighbourhood,
Who you gonna call? Ghostbusters!
If there's something weird, and it don't look good,
Who you gonna call? Ghostbusters!'*[53]

The phrase has become an addition to our modern-day vernacular. Often if someone says, 'who are you going to call?', the other person will reply with 'Ghostbusters'. The next three chapters are looking at nine 'Joy Busters': worry, fear, shame, guilt, comparison, disappointment, toxic thinking, un-forgiveness, and bad attitudes.

Who we gonna call? Jesus! He is the restorer of our joy.

First, a quick recap.

1. We have an enemy of our souls, the devil. He is out to steal and destroy our joy and all the other elements of the abundant life Jesus came to give.

    'The thief does not come except to steal, and to kill, and to destroy. I have come that they may have life, and that they may have it more abundantly.'—John 10:10

2. We find the keys to retaining joy are abiding or dwelling in the love of Jesus and keeping His commands. His commands are His words in the Bible, His words to live by.

    'As the Father loved Me, I also have loved you; abide in My love. If you keep My commandments, you will abide in My love, just as I have kept My Father's commandments and abide in His love.

These things I have spoken to you, that My joy may remain in you, and that your joy may be full.'—John 15:9-11

3. Staying close to the source of joy, so close it's the place we live from, releases fullness of joy that remains. We do this by knowing His love intimately and living from a place of accepting His deep love. When we live by His commands, by His words, joy remains.

'You will show me the path of life; in Your presence is fullness of joy; At Your right hand are pleasures forevermore.'—Psalm 16:11

Now let's dive into the first three challenges that steal and 'bust' our joy.

Joy Buster 1: Worry

'Worry is a cycle of inefficient thoughts whirling around a centre of fear.'—Corrie ten Boom

This quote conjures images of a whirling vortex tornado and is the opposite of the peace and joy that Jesus offers. So, what does worry actually do?

- Worry will keep your mind so busy that it cannot contain any joy.
- Worry will take up your head space so there is no room for gratitude or any thoughts that will bring joy.
- Worry will have free reign and consume your thinking if you let it.

I used to be quite an expert at worrying. I did not know I could be proactive about my thinking, so worry would just come and go as it pleased. Worry is often nocturnal; it does not think you deserve to sleep well. Worry likes to rob your sleep, peace, and joy.

About three years after we started Lighthouse Church, there was a period of a few big issues we had to deal with. I was losing a lot of sleep which I desperately needed with two small, high-energy boys so I asked God to help me.

As God often does when we seek Him, He gave me a deep revelation and conviction. He pointed out that He had said: 'Do not worry' and this was, in fact, a command, not a suggestion. I realised in that moment that I had begun to worry and not follow this command, which in turn was affecting my sleep.

> *'... do not worry about tomorrow, for tomorrow will worry about itself. Each day has enough trouble of its own.'—Matthew 6:34 (NLT)*

He reminded me of something I knew to be true in other areas of my life when He said this. When He asks something of us, He will also supply the empowering and enabling. He reminded me that repenting enables His empowering. As we acknowledge our own way is not right, this enables Him to empower us. So, I repented of worrying. I prayed: *'Sorry for worrying and not trusting You, Jesus. Please, Holy Spirit come and empower me to stop worrying and release your peace and joy.'*

He answered my prayer and brought a significant breakthrough in this area in my life. I still worry at times, but it doesn't have the same power on me as it did previously. When worry does creep in, I again repent and ask for God's peace and joy in place of the worry.

Jesus can provide a similar breakthrough for you if you will bring your cares (or worries) to Him.

Then Jesus said, 'Come to me, all of you who are weary and carry heavy burdens, and I will give you rest. Take my yoke upon you. Let me teach you, because I am humble and gentle at heart, and you will find rest for your souls. For my yoke is easy to bear, and the burden I give you is light.'—Matthew 11: 28-30 (NLT)

God's gift of the present

Remember this about worry: it will try to bring you too far into the future and into futile areas which you cannot control. It will also try to bring you into the past to ruminate about the details of a scene over and over. In order to evict worry, it is important to stay in the moment and do as Jesus said: 'Do not worry about tomorrow.'

'If you're not careful to think and speak words of faith, worry will creep in, and it will not only steal your peace and joy, it will steal your 'today.' The present is the greatest gift God ever gives us. So, hold on to the peace that's yours in Christ. Don't let it go.' —Joyce Meyer

When my parents developed dementia, my mind would try to go into the future and worry about how it would all play out. Would they forget me altogether? Would they live so long that they'd end up in a bed being spoon fed? How would they pass away? How long would I have to endure watching them slip away into shadows of themselves? During this time, it became crucial to stay in the present. The rest was unknown and out of my hands. The present was where I could create some precious moments with my parents to treasure as memories after they'd gone.

It wasn't always easy, and I had to remind myself continually to stay in the moment. When I could do that, it enabled me to find creative ideas of how to make the most of the time I still had with them. Even the difficult things became a joy when I stayed in the present. I remember clipping their fingernails for them and helping them with their food. It was both a great sadness that my parents could no longer do this for themselves, mingled with a great joy of being able to bless them in this intimate way. When I stayed in worry, however, I was too weighed down to think of anything creative to do with them and I was too worn down to have anything to give. Staying in the present kept me sane and able to stay afloat.

Don Joseph Goewey, author of The End of Stress, Four Steps to Rewire Your Brian, wrote an article that cites a study showing what a waste of time most of our worry truly is.

> *'Five hundred years ago, Michel de Montaigne said: 'My life has been filled with terrible misfortune; most of which never happened.' Now there's a study that proves it. This study looked into how many of our imagined calamities never materialise. In this study, subjects were asked to write down their worries over an extended period of time and then identify which of their imagined misfortunes did not actually happen. Lo and behold, it turns out that 85 percent of what*

subjects worried about never happened, and with the 15 percent that did happen, 79 percent of subjects discovered either they could handle the difficulty better than expected, or the difficulty taught them a lesson worth learning. This means that 97 percent of what you worry over is not much more than a fearful mind punishing you with exaggerations and misperceptions.[54]

Decide *now* to not allow worry to steal your joy. Accept God's gift of the present and remind yourself to live there. Ask God to empower you to obey His words: 'Do not worry.'

Joy Buster 2: Fear

Fear is one of the biggest threats to joy. Fear paralyses and binds us. It puts us in prison and forces us to cower and hide.

I want to clarify here that there are three types of fear: **warning** fear, **reverential** fear, and **adverse** fear.

Warning fear, as I call it, is a good kind of fear that basically warns us of imminent danger or threat. Reverential fear is a holy fear of our all-mighty, all-powerful, God. Adverse fear busts our joy by binding us in anxiety (worry) and fear of the future.

Recognising adverse fear

God knows we are susceptible to this adverse kind of fear. So much so, He instructs us to 'fear not' 365 times throughout the Bible, enough for each day of the year.

Adverse fear has a language. It sounds like this: What if? What if I make a mistake? What if nothing works out? What if they laugh at me? What if I don't know what to say or do? What if I don't have enough? What if I get sick? This questioning and fear loop then essentially causes a mental block which paralyses us and robs our joy.

Adverse fear has been a close acquaintance in my life. Through the power of Jesus, I have overcome many fears with some still in process.

One I decided I'd keep; the fear of heights. I decided this one is not interfering with my life too much. Interesting the cover design features a hot air balloon; perhaps I will conquer that fear one day!

Adverse fear, like what we are discussing here, is almost always irrational. The well know acronym '**F**alse **E**xpectations **A**ppearing **R**eal', is a great reminder of what it really is: even though the fear is irrational, and when present seems very real, it generally turns out to be a false perspective, wasting much of our time, energy and capacity and drawing us away from living above this joy buster.

Adverse fear is a spirit, according to 2 Timothy 1:7: 'For God has not given us a *spirit* of fear, but of power and of love and of a sound mind.' (emphasis added), and Romans 8:14-15:

> *'For as many as are led by the Spirit of God, these are sons of God. For you did not **receive the spirit of bondage** again to fear, but you **received the Spirit of adoption** by whom we cry out, 'Abba, Father.'' (emphasis added).*

Love: God's secret weapon to expelling fear

We have a God-given spirit of love, not fear. But how often does fear try to take over? God has given us a sound mind, but fear tries to play tricks on our mind and deceive us.

So how do we overcome fear? By tapping into the great and limitless reservoir of God's love.

> *'There is no fear in love [dread does not exist]. But perfect (complete, full-grown) love drives out fear, because fear involves [the expectation of divine] punishment, so the one who is afraid [of God's judgment] is not perfected in love [has not grown into a sufficient understanding of God's love]. We love because He first loved us.'—1 John 19-4:18 (AMP)*

I love this passage because I know first-hand that it's true. His perfect love has driven out so much fear in my life.

It is such an amazing and powerful passage. When we have a deep understanding of God's love, fear cannot stay. When fear comes, we need to go to God for a new understanding of His love so the fear can be driven out.

The love of God will mean something different for all of us, and that is the beautiful thing about it. Here are some wonderful declarations to remind yourself of:

- God's love is so vast and so indescribable, yet entirely personal to me.
- It is so beyond our wildest imagination and understanding, yet so available and attainable for us.
- God's love is so multi-faceted, that there are enough facets of His love to last us a whole lifetime of new revelations and applications.

The beauty of His love is that it never gets tired. God's love is never old news. His love is unfailing. His love is unconditional. His love accepts us as we are, but loves us too much to leave us there. His love is never something to move on from or grow out of.

God made us for love and to be in perfect love union with Him. The fall in Genesis 2 robbed us of that, and the enemy of our souls continues to try to rob us of knowing, really knowing, the love of God.

We can never fully know in our human capacity the height, depth, width, and length of His love. But it is like a journey where you don't have to get to the end to get the benefit of it. The prize of the quest is found in each step. Every time we get a deeper glimpse into His love, we are strengthened even if we can never understand all of it.

It is in His incredible love that fear is expelled.

> *'... the love of God has been poured out in our hearts by the Holy Spirit who was given to us.'*—Romans 5:5

> Ask God to pour His love into your heart by His Holy Spirit. Ask Him to give you a fresh and deeper understanding of His love and to keep pouring His love into you until your fear is prevented from robbing your joy.

The good fear I mentioned earlier—the reverential fear of God, also displaces adverse fear. A good way to fear God in this way is to worship Him. There are many inspired songs that describe the greatness of God and ascribe worth to Him. Or worship Him by praying and speaking out how great He is. A read through the Psalms will reveal many passages of ascribing greatness to God.

Declaring God's word eradicates fear

> *"Fear of the Lord' is the deeply sane recognition that we are not God. How long since you felt this fear? Since a fresh understanding of Christ buckled your knees and emptied your lungs? Since a glimpse of him left you speechless and breathless? If it's been a while, that explains your fears. When Christ is great, our fears are not.'—Max Lucado*

One way to keep God and His Word front and centre so that our fear does not have any opportunity, is to declare His Word over our fear.

We saw in Chapter 3 that God's Word is living and active and as sharp as a sword. One way to wield this sword is to speak it out loud. That way the devil can hear the powerful Word of God. He is not God so cannot hear our thoughts but can hear what we say out loud. The Bible also tells us that there is great power in what we say.

> *'Death and life are in the power of the tongue ... '*
> *—Proverbs 18:21*

Furthermore, when God speaks, He accomplishes and prospers that which He has spoken.

> *'So shall My word be that goes forth from My mouth; it shall not return to Me void, but it shall accomplish what I please, and it shall prosper in the thing for which I sent it.'—Isaiah 55:11*

I have had some big breakthroughs with fear when I declared the truth of God's Word out loud. It was usually a process over time, establishing and re-establishing God's truth over my fears.

Sometimes we are so entrenched in patterns of thinking related to our fears that a process is needed to unravel those patterns, so be encouraged and press into God as you work through this joy buster.

Recognising fear's bedfellow: Intimidation

An example of having to press in continually to overcome fear in my life was in the area of intimidation. I had severe back pain issues when I was younger. When there was a call for healing, I would often ask for prayer for healing for my back. One day, some people prayed for me and sensed a spirit of intimidation. When they prayed for Jesus to deliver me from a spirit of intimidation, my back improved significantly, and I felt less intimidated around people for a while. The intimidation would often come back, however, and it was not until I made a habit of declaring God's Word over my life that it came back less and less often. I would declare this: 'For God has not given [me] a spirit of fear and timidity, but of power, love, and [a sound mind].' 2 Timothy 1:7 (NLT)

I also read John Bevere's book, Breaking Intimidation[55]. As I read, I could almost feel my thought patterns unravelling and God opening my mind to overcoming this insidious bedfellow of fear.

Overcoming this type of fear required a three-phrase approach: prayer, declaring God's Word and renewing my mind. I am pleased to say that I feel less intimidated than ever before, although it does rear its ugly head from time to time. If there is an area of fear where you are not finding victory, perhaps look into this three-phrase approach I have just outlined. I believe God has the power to deliver instantaneously, and sometimes He does. Other times, He wants to hold our hand and journey with us through a process.

If fear is busting your joy, here are some steps to follow:

1. Be aware of annoying 'what if' thoughts which stem from fear.
2. Ask God for a deeper revelation of His love and for His Spirit to pour His love into your heart.
3. Worship God in reverential awe. As the reverential fear of how great He is grows, the adverse fear shrinks.
4. Find a passage in the Bible that speaks into your fear and declare it out loud on a regular basis.
5. Renew your mind and thought patterns relating to this fear.
6. Ask a trusted leader or friend to pray for release from a spirit of fear.

Joy Buster 3: Shame

Everlasting joy is the promise when shame is released from our lives.

> *'Instead of your shame you shall have double honour, and instead of confusion they shall rejoice in their portion. Therefore, in their land they shall possess double; everlasting joy shall be theirs.'—Isaiah 61:7 NKJV*

There is a course by Careforce Lifekeys called Search for Life[56], developed by Dr Allan Meyer. I led this a few times in our church in Sydney. One video is about guilt and shame, and Dr Meyer speaks about the difference between the two.

Guilt is linked to a wrong action and comes from sin when you have done something wrong and your conscience troubles you. Shame is more insidious. Shame makes us feel 'not enough'.

Dr Meyer defines it as:

> *'Shame is like a glob of unworthiness that sticks to the human soul and brings with it emotional distress and feelings of hopelessness.'*[57]

This is a definite joy buster. It is difficult to maintain joy with emotional distress and hopelessness. Feeling unworthy robs our joy; however, there is joy in living the life God intended for you when He created you. It is that feeling of flourishing in all you were created for.

> C. S. Lewis says, 'I sometimes think that shame, mere awkward, senseless shame, does as much towards preventing good acts and straightforward happiness as any of our vices can do.'[58]

That glob of unworthiness in fact stops good acts and happiness. It stops us from fulfilling the good acts God has prepared for us. We know from Chapter 5 that if we are prevented from purpose, we lose our joy.

The origins of shame

The origins of shame are in the fall of mankind. First of all, God made all of nature and animals and looked at His creation and said it was good. He then created human beings, and this time He said it was very good.

> 'Then God said, 'Let us make human beings in our image, to be like us' ... then God looked over all he had made, and he saw that it was very good.' —Genesis 1:26,31 (NLT)

So, all was very good and then came tragedy.

> 'The serpent was the shrewdest of all the wild animals the Lord God had made. One day he asked the woman, 'Did God really say you must not eat the fruit from any of the trees in the garden?'

> 'Of course, we may eat fruit from the trees in the garden,' the woman replied. 'It's only the fruit from the tree in the middle of the garden that we are not allowed to eat. God said, 'You must not eat it or even touch it; if you do, you will die.' 'You won't die!' the serpent replied to the woman. 'God knows that your eyes will be opened as soon as you eat it, and you will be like God, knowing both good and evil.'

> The woman was convinced. She saw that the tree was beautiful, and its fruit looked delicious, and she wanted the wisdom it would give her. So, she took some of the fruit and ate it. Then she gave some to her husband, who was with her, and he ate it, too. At that moment, their eyes were opened, and they suddenly felt shame at their nakedness. So,

they sewed fig leaves together to cover themselves. When the cool evening breezes were blowing, the man and his wife heard the Lord God walking about in the garden. So, they hid from the Lord God among the trees.'—Genesis 3:1-8 (NLT)

The serpent, the devil, came and put doubt in Eve's mind that she wasn't good enough. She didn't have what it takes; she needed to be like God and have more wisdom and knowledge, so he tempted her to eat of the fruit of that tree. The enemy put a slur on who God made her to be. God said, 'very good', the devil said, 'not good enough'. So, she gave in and sin ended perfection.

At that point, Adam and Eve's eyes were opened to shame; they felt naked, so found some fig leaves to cover the dreadful sense of physical, emotional, and spiritual nakedness. They felt exposed, so they hid. Shame makes you want to hide and withdraw. Shame makes you want to isolate.

Shame has its place in the story of redemption by highlighting how desperately we need a Saviour. But when left unchecked, it lies to us and tells us we are not enough even when we stand in the fullness of right relationship and right standing with God through Jesus Christ. Experiencing shame serves a destructive purpose if it causes us to cower and hide.

Lift up your head

There is a verse I love in Psalm 34. It has spoken to me over the years and is foundational to my testimony.

> *'I prayed to the Lord, and he answered me. He freed me from all my fears. Those who look to him for help will be radiant with joy; no shadow of shame will darken their faces.'—Psalm 34:4-5*

Shame can cast a shadow and darken our countenance. There is an expression: 'she hung her head in shame'. Shame causes us to be downcast and look down, but this Psalm encourages us to look up. To look up at our Father God and allow His Presence to bring radiant joy in the place of shame. It is helpful to symbolically, physically look up.

The Psalmist even tells us that God lifts our head.

> 'But You, O Lord, are a shield for me, my glory, and the lifter of my head.'—Psalm 3:3 (AMPC)

Picture your loving Father God holding your face in His hands and saying to you, 'look to Me and you'll be radiant, look to Me and I'll lift your head'. Rather than cowering in shame, look up to Him in worship. For confidence and approval, look up at Him.

If shame has come to you by abuse or another traumatic experience, please reach out to a wise, trusted friend who can pray with you and journey with you. It may be helpful for some with deep shame to reach out to a Christian counsellor who is skilled to bring the healing of Jesus to you.

Why don't you pray the words of Psalm 34 now and personalise it to include your specific fears and shame?

Joy Buster 4: Guilt

Joy comes from being freed from guilt. It is the most amazing news we will ever hear. The Lord has cleared us of guilt through the sacrifice of Jesus Christ on the cross and by the power of His resurrection.

> 'Yes, what joy for those whose record the Lord has cleared of guilt, whose lives are lived in complete honesty!'—Psalm 32:2 (NLT)

> 'There is now no condemnation [no guilty verdict, no punishment] for those who are in Christ Jesus [who believe in Him as personal Lord and Saviour]. For the law of the Spirit of life [which is] in Christ Jesus [the law of our new being] has set you free from the law of sin and of death.'—Romans 8:1-2 AMP

Through Jesus, we are declared righteous and our standing in God is a 'not guilty' verdict, hallelujah! If you have a sense of never-ending guilt, it is not from God. If this is the case for you, please read through Romans 8 and Ephesians 1 to 3. Let your mind be renewed by the grace and assurance we have as soon as we decide to turn our lives over to Jesus as our Lord and Saviour.

Breaking the cycle

We do, however, still do the wrong thing at times. We still sin this side of eternity. The guilt that comes from our conscience when we sin should be more like a conviction than a condemnation. It is a matter of the Holy Spirit convicting us of wrongdoing and then forgiving us and empowering us to turn away from the sin and walk in the right way. It is a quick prompting with a desire to do better empowered by the Holy Spirit. If it is like a feeling of condemnation with no hope of ever doing any better and no hope of being forgiven or empowered to do better, then it is not from God.

> '... sin is one of the sneakiest joy thieves... sin has an extremely destructive ripple effect in your life. It impacts the people around you and it destroys your ability to experience the joy and peace God has for you... Make the decision today that you will not let ANYTHING get between you and this joy-filled life God has for you. If you've been making poor choices, lift your eyes to God. Let His love, acceptance and forgiveness set you free. His power is in you to change and become strong against whatever is tempting you so you can live free in His joy!'[59]—Leon Fontaine

Sin lures and tempts you and lies that it will bring joy and happiness. Sin can also trap you into a cycle which is difficult to break free from. The guilt will then lie to you that you are too sinful to go to God. In fact, the opposite is true. Run *to* God, not *from* God! He is waiting with open arms to love you, forgive you and free you from the sin that is binding you.

> 'The Son radiates God's own glory and expresses the very character of God, and He sustains everything by the mighty power of His command. When He had cleansed us from our sins, He sat down in the place of honour at the right hand of the majestic God in heaven.'—Hebrews 1:3 (NLT)

On the cross Jesus declared; 'It is finished.' (John 19:30). He appeared to many after His resurrection and then ascended to heaven and sat down with His mission of redemption completed.

Do not allow the enemy of your soul to rob your joy. Do not allow him to tempt you to carry on sinning and not going to God for forgiveness and victory over the sin. Do not allow him to lie to you that you are not forgiven and place a false burden of guilt on your shoulders to carry around. Either way, there is freedom in Jesus Christ.

Selah: stop, connect, enjoy ...

What is busting your joy?

Meditate on this passage and ponder how it can stop worry and restore joy in your life. Ask God to empower you to obey this passage.

> '... do not worry about tomorrow, for tomorrow will worry about itself. Each day has enough trouble of its own.'—Matthew 6:34 (NLT)

In which areas of your life would it be helpful to live in the present, the moment? What thought processes need to change to do this?

If fear is busting your joy, here are some steps to follow:

- Be aware of annoying 'what if' thoughts which stem from fear.
- Ask God for a deeper revelation of His love and for His Spirit to pour His love into your heart.
- Worship God in reverential awe. As the good fear of how great He is grows, the adverse fear shrinks.
- Find a passage in the Bible that speaks into your fear and declare it out loud on a regular basis.
- Renew your mind and thought patterns relating to the fear.
- Ask a trusted leader or friend to pray for release from a spirit of fear.

Is there a hint of shame that is busting joy in your life?

Meditate on this passage and ask God to reveal to you any areas in which He wants to set you free.

> 'I prayed to the Lord, and he answered me. He freed me from all my fears. Those who look to him for help will be radiant with joy; no shadow of shame will darken their faces.'—Psalm 34:4-5

Picture your loving Father God holding your face in His hands and saying to you, 'look to Me and you'll be radiant, look to Me and I'll lift your head'.

Rather than cowering in shame, look up to Him in worship. For confidence and approval, look up at Him.

Is there an area of sin that you are finding hard to overcome? Have a conversation with God about it and ask for His forgiveness and His help to conquer.

Are you carrying false guilt? Bring it to Jesus by asking Him to release you from this burden.

8. JOY Busters: Comparison & Disappointment

Joy Buster 5: Comparison

'Comparison is the thief of joy.'—President Theodore Roosevelt

Comparison will push you into a corner where there is no joy. It will produce painful insecurity, trigger debilitating feelings of inadequacy and shift your focus from your calling to self-absorption.

Comparison will rob you of the life God created you for to live. Never satisfied, comparison says, *you'll never be as good as them or you're going to have to work harder to be better than them* and so on. Who can ever 'be good enough' when measured with 'others'? We were not created to be 'others' so will never measure up. This is because we use our weaknesses versus the strengths of others as our measuring stick instead of measuring ourselves only by the word of God. And there is no joy to be found (or contentment in who we are in Christ) in falling short due to using a faulty measure.

You can either be intimidated or ask God: 'What do you want me to say and do in the way you made me, with my unique, God-given design'?

It can be hard when you are around exceptionally talented people, or even people you want to be like, but the choice is yours.

All of us, every person on earth: young and old, introvert and extrovert, calm and fiery, funny, and serious, methodical, and creative, ordered and spontaneous, have a contribution to make in our own distinctive way.

'Be yourself; everyone else is already taken!'[60]—*Oscar Wilde*

Every person on the planet is created for a unique purpose with unique strengths and unique weaknesses. Every single personality type has strengths *and* corresponding weaknesses—no-one is immune to having both.

All comparison of strengths and weaknesses will rob joy. Often we measure my weaknesses versus their strengths. However, if the measuring stick is their weaknesses versus my strengths, that is also an unhealthy comparison which aims for 'one-upmanship' and will certainly bust joy.

We are all different, and it is a waste of God's time for us to compare ourselves with others. Rather, let us go to Him and ask Him what He uniquely wants *me* to do and say and be.

The dangers of social media comparison

There is another form of comparison that has surfaced in the last few years. Social media has generated comparison at devastating new levels. People are comparing their own reality, with everyone else's perceived reality. Rarely do you see a post of someone's worst moments unless they are funny. If viewed with no wisdom, it is easy for people to compare other people's seemingly perfect lives with what they perceive to be their own 'far from perfect' life.

The other, not so obvious, form of comparison is people comparing their 'real life' with their own social media persona. It is easy for people to set up a dazzling, perfect, digital image. When their actual life does not compare with their perceived and preferred image of themselves, it can produce disappointment with themselves and loss of joy and even significantly impact their mental health and real-world relationships.

Stay in your lane

It's not uncommon to hear someone say that they have a right to compare—that they've had a hard go of things when others have not, and that they deserve to have more because of it. Nick Vujicic, Christian evangelist, and motivational speaker has every reason to compare. Born with tetra-amelia syndrome, he has no arms and legs and almost everyone else on earth does! He says this about being all God designed him to be:

> *'I found happiness when I realised that as imperfect as I may be, I am the perfect Nick Vujicic. I am God's creation, designed according to His plan for me. That's not to say there isn't room for improvement. I'm always trying to be better so I can better serve Him and the world!'*

Despite his limitations, Nick is walking in God's plan for his life. He has travelled around the world and shared his story with millions, sometimes in stadiums filled to capacity, speaking to a range of diverse groups such as students, teachers, young people, business professionals and church congregations of all sizes. Today this dynamic evangelist has accomplished more than most people achieve in a lifetime. He's an author, musician, actor, husband, and father and his hobbies include fishing, painting, and swimming.[61]

All without arms and legs!

This demonstrates there are no limitations to walking in all God has purposed for us. There are, however, limitations to walking in a life God has purposed for someone else.

There is a phrase that has become prominent in recent times: 'Stay in your lane'. The Bible puts it this way:

> '... let us run with endurance the race that is set before us ... '
> —Hebrews 12:1

Stay in our lane in the race God has given us to run. Not the race He has given *someone else* to run.

Comparison can also affect the way we see and comprehend God's love for us. If I were, 'as good as her or did as much as her' then God would love me more. Not true!

Here are some more 'not true' statements you may have heard others, or even yourself, express:

God must love that person more than me because they have better talents, the ones I want instead of mine!

God must love them more because they have more finances, talents, friends, family, _____ than me.

God must love them more because they are kinder, humbler, and more loving than me.

These are all lies. This is what the Bible says about God's intimate knowledge, love, and care towards each one of us individually.

> *'For You formed my inward parts; You covered me in my mother's womb. I will praise You, for I am fearfully and wonderfully made; marvellous are Your works, and that my soul knows very well. My frame was not hidden from You, when I was made in secret, and skilfully wrought in the lowest parts of the earth. Your eyes saw my substance, being yet unformed. And in Your book they all were written, the days fashioned for me, when as yet there were none of them. How precious also are Your thoughts to me, O God! How great is the sum of them! If I should count them, they would be more in number than the sand... '—Psalm 139:13-18*

That is astounding! The God who created the entire universe has precious thoughts towards me which total more than the number of grains of sand at every beach on the planet! That is a lot of thoughts! More than enough to last a entire lifetime, I would estimate.

The wonder of being known

Another astounding truth we find in this passage is He has fashioned my days for me before I was even born. He has a book for me where He has written my life story. I have the choice whether to walk in His life story for me or my own inferior version. I reckon I can say quite confidently that His version will be the best one!

The NLT (New Living Translation) version of the Bible says that every moment was laid out. God has laid out an abundant life each day for each one of us. If we combine the NLT and NKJV (New King James Version) versions, we could use the analogy that God has laid out for us what to wear each day (*not physically, although sometimes that too! Jesus said not to worry about what to wear and He's provided me with some fabulous gifts in terms of clothing!*)

Here is how God has asked us to clothe ourselves.

> *'Clothe yourself with the presence of the Lord Jesus Christ.'*
> *—Romans 13:14 (NLT)*

> *'Since God chose you to be the holy people he loves, you must clothe yourselves with tender-hearted mercy, kindness, humility, gentleness, and patience ... Above all, clothe yourselves with love ...'—Colossian 3:12, 14 (NLT)*

None of these 'clothes' allow for comparison. If we are clothed in love and are kind, gentle and patient, we will not be comparing but celebrating. We will be celebrating the differences between us. We will be celebrating if someone else is doing well and celebrating the diversity and successes of others.

Comparison can stem from having an 'orphan spirit'. An orphan spirit is present when we do not have a true understanding of our identity as a son or daughter of God through Christ Jesus. If we are not secure in this new identity, we have through Christ Jesus, it is hard to receive God's love and acceptance. When we don't know we are loved and accepted, we feel inferior and consequently compare ourselves to others.

Here is the truth of who we are from God's Word.

> *'Behold what manner of love the Father has bestowed on us, that we should be called children of God!'—1 John 3:1*

> *'For as many as are led by the Spirit of God, these are sons of God. For you did not receive the spirit of bondage again to fear, but you received the Spirit of adoption by whom we cry out, 'Abba, Father.' The Spirit Himself bears witness with our spirit that we are children of God, and if children,*

> then heirs—heirs of God and joint heirs with Christ, if indeed we suffer with Him, that we may also be glorified together.'—Romans 8:14-17

We are children of the Most High God! Allow that to blow your mind for a moment. God chose us. He chose to adopt us. It wasn't a mistake or accident. God loved us so much that He purposely sent His only son Jesus to suffer terribly on that cruel cross in our place so that we could be adopted as His children. If we truly have a revelation of this, the point of comparison becomes null and void. His table is big enough for us all!

> 'To live as God's child is to know, at this very instant, that you are loved by your Maker not because you try to please him and succeed, or fail to please him and apologise, but because he wants to be your Father. Nothing more. All your efforts to win his affection are unnecessary. All your fears of losing his affection are needless. You can no more make him want you than you can convince him to abandon you. The adoption is irreversible. You have a place at his table.' —Max Lucado

Judgement: the underbelly of comparison

Comparison can also be a form of judgement. If I am comparing, then I essentially judge that you are either superior or inferior to me. God is unambiguous about judging.

> 'Judge not, and you shall not be judged.'
> —Luke 6:37

When you judge, it turns back on you. This dawned on me when my boys were little. I had never made it to university and had some regrets about this. We lived in an area where most people were highly educated with successful careers. I felt inferior to the other parents.

One day, God showed me I was actually judging them—that they would be the type of people to judge me. He showed me how this passage was true of my own heart. Because He opened my eyes and I changed my thinking, I gained some wonderful friends who were much more educated than me and I was able to celebrate their successes. If I had continued with my destructive judging and comparison, I would have missed out on the joy of having those friendships and being free in them.

Comparison really is a conniving thief of joy. So, let's leave comparison alone. Let's get on with the joy of celebrating our diversity. Let's get on with celebrating the successes of others. Let's get on with the joy of living the pages in that book that God has fashioned for us.

Joy Buster 6: Disappointment

'Repeated disappointment almost always triggers a series of other reactions: discouragement, anger, frustration, bitterness, resentment, even depression. Unless we learn to deal with disappointment, it will rob us of joy and poison our souls.'[62] —Billy Graham

What is disappointment? The dictionary meaning is: 'Sadness or displeasure caused by the non-fulfilment of one's hopes or expectations.'[63]

Psychologists describe the feeling of disappointment: 'As an emotion, researchers describe disappointment as a form of sadness—a feeling of loss, an uncomfortable space (or a painful gap) between our expectations and reality.'[64]

Disappointment visits us all. Some disappointment is almost unbearable while other disappointments are a minor setback or annoyance. Sometimes disappointment challenges our belief system or motivates a desire to give up, withdraw or run away. Disappointment often precipitates grief and anger, and can lead us into bitterness, disillusionment, and weariness. One thing is clear: disappointment will *always* bust our joy.

Disappointment was a major contributor to my loss of joy. A number of disappointments over time gradually wore me down. I can relate to almost everything in Billy Graham's quote above.

Disappointment from unmet expectations

One day I went for a walk and was crying out to God. He whispered into my spirit, 'expectation comes from Me, come to Me for your expectations and let go of the expectations that are not from Me'. I got back from my walk and looked up what the Bible had to say about expectations.

'My soul, wait only upon God and silently submit to Him; for my hope and expectation are from Him.' Psalm 62:5 (AMPC) In fact, the whole of Psalm 62 speaks into the place of disappointment.

This passage is yet another example of David speaking to and directing his soul, as he often did. He led himself, led his soul, into waiting on God and submitting to God and sourcing his hope and expectation from God, rather than from his own expectations.

This led me on a journey to revisit my expectations that had not been met and question if they were, in fact, unreasonable expectations. I asked God to adjust my expectations to line up with His.

Keeping a journal was immensely helpful for me during this time. I made a list of my expectations and then began sorting, such as when you declutter your wardrobe. I had to sort my expectations. Some expectations had to go into the trash. Some were set aside to be re-purposed, some were to keep just as they were, and others needed a bit of alteration.

The reason disappointment is insidious is that it can cause us to question what we believe; what our worldview is; the lens through which we see the world. Sometimes this is helpful as it brings us to a deeper understanding of something we may have believed that was not quite right or a bit distorted. Other times it can be disturbing when we realise we do not believe what is true.

I remember being devastated one day when I realised I didn't really, in my hearts of hearts, believe God is always good. I thought I did. The Bible says He is, and I believe the Bible is the absolute truth. I believed in my head that God is good all the time, and I knew without a doubt *in my head* that this is the truth. However, in my *heart*, because of disappointments, I was not grasping this as a truth for my life. I knew He was good but not necessarily that He wanted to be good to me personally. It took some time to unravel my thinking process around this and many encounters with God where He gently showed me His goodness and revealed to me that He is always 'for me'.

Christine Caine said this of the COVID-19 season:

> *'Many of us are walking through major disappointments in this season. So many losses, unrealised plans and dreams, people letting us down, and of course, us letting others down. Disappointment is real, painful and can be debilitating. The Enemy wants us to stay stuck in our disappointment in hopes that we will miss future God appointments.*
>
> *One of the hardest things we must learn to do is to deal with and move beyond our disappointments and failures. On the other side of the *DIS* is an *APPOINTMENT*—and that appointment could change yours or someone else's life.*
>
> *The current chapter of your life may be a long one, but your story is not over yet. Though the unexpected happens, God never leaves you there. Keep trusting. Keep believing. 'For it is God who is working in you both to will and to work according to his good purpose.'—Philippians 2:13*[85]

Writing this book is an example of an appointment on the other side of a disappointment. If I hadn't walked through disappointment and experienced a loss of joy, I would not have had any authentic material to work from.

Everything looks great in hindsight

I can think of many other examples in my life where **disappointments** have been turned into **appointments**. The problem is you do not know this until hindsight is available.

> *When you are in the middle of disappointment, you need to make the decision to overcome. Otherwise it will sink you and poison your soul. You need to draw near to God and wait on Him and get your expectation from Him.*

It can also be helpful to read stories of other people who have overcome disappointments to build up your faith and hope. One such person is Joni Eareckson Tada, who became a quadriplegic as a result of a diving accident at the age of seventeen. She founded Joni and Friends in 1979 to provide Christ-centred ministry to special-needs families, as well as training for churches. Joni and Friends serves thousands of special-needs families through Family Retreats and has delivered over 170,000 wheelchairs and Bibles to needy individuals with disabilities in developing nations.[66]

Joni says this about finding joy through disappointment and suffering—

> *'Many people in the throes of suffering, disappointment, and despair, feel utterly stuck in their circumstances. They see no hope beyond their day-to-day drudgery of disability routines; but when hurting families place themselves under the shower of God's mercy, suddenly the clouds part. They realise there's hope, life, and even joy beyond their suffering.'*[67]

As well as circumstances, another source of disappointment is other people. We have certain expectations on others, perhaps based on the expectations we have on ourselves or expectations based on our world-view. We expect others to comply and when they don't, we can experience disappointment. This is an insight from my husband on dealing with this particular area of disappointment:

> *'We live in a village. In this village, there are many differing world-views to ours. In order to live in the village, we have to adapt and adjust our expectations to avoid frustration, keep our peace and live in joy. The alternative is to live on an island alone. We need to live in the tension; keep our worldview whilst understanding others have their worldview.'*—Paul Zanardo, Pastor

Disappointment generally comes down to expectations. When it comes to others, a good question to ask is: 'what are my expectations on this person and are they realistic?' If you still think the expectations are realistic, then it is a matter of accepting that every person has to make their own decisions and has their own worldview, and we cannot change anyone. We can only change our own response to them. That is when Godly character comes in and we need to choose kindness, forgiveness, gentleness, and long-suffering love.

When we are the source of our disappointment

It's hard but true: we can often have much higher expectations on ourselves than on anyone else. This can stem from a tendency to perfectionism, unreasonably expecting that we will never make mistakes. It can also come from performance mentality where we believe that we only have worth if we perform exceptionally well or believing that we must continually grow and improve and never go backwards.

There are many good goals to aim for and it is good to aim to avoid mistakes, to do well in all we put our hand to. It is good to have a growth mindset and aim to improve ourselves physically, emotionally, and spiritually. The unhelpful, joy-depleting disappointment comes into play if we are so rigid in these expectations that we find it difficult to cope when we do not meet them.

Sometimes I have found it helpful to 'talk to myself' as David did throughout the Psalms. If your own expectations are much higher on yourself than others, try talking to yourself as if you were talking to a friend and challenge the perfectionistic, 'no room to fail' thinking.

Let's do a little character study on Peter, the apostle and disciple of Jesus. He experienced three sources of disappointment: disappointment with Jesus, disappointment with others, and disappointment with himself.

> *Jesus began to tell his disciples plainly that it was necessary for him to go to Jerusalem, and that he would suffer many terrible things at the hands of the elders, the leading priests, and the teachers of religious law. He would be killed, but on the third day he would be raised from the*

dead. But Peter took him aside and began to reprimand him for saying such things. 'Heaven forbid, Lord,' he said. 'This will never happen to you!' Jesus turned to Peter and said, 'Get away from me, Satan! You are a dangerous trap to me. You are seeing things merely from a human point of view, not from God's."—Matthew 16: 21-23 (NLT)

Peter was so disappointed with God's plan that he had the audacity to rebuke and disagree with Jesus, the son of God. The disciples and all the Jews had been expecting the Messiah would come and conquer the Roman Empire by force. God had a bigger picture: to conquer the devil's empire of evil, sin, pain, and death.

When Peter expressed his disappointment with the plan, Jesus reprimanded him quite harshly for his human viewpoint rather than seeing the plan from God's view. Is it possible you may be viewing some of your areas of disappointment from the wrong perspective? Take a moment to ask God what his viewpoint is on the matter.

Secondly, Peter was disappointed with James and John along with the other disciples when he listened to their requests to Jesus.

> *'Then James and John, the sons of Zebedee, came to Him, saying, "Teacher, we want You to do for us whatever we ask." And He said to them, "What do you want Me to do for you?". They said to Him, "Grant us that we may sit, one on Your right hand and the other on Your left, in Your glory." But Jesus said to them, "You do not know what you ask. Are you able to drink the cup that I drink, and be baptised with the baptism that I am baptised with?"... And when the ten heard it, they began to be greatly displeased with James and John.*
>
> *But Jesus called them to Himself and said to them, "You know that those who are considered rulers over the Gentiles lord it over them, and their great ones exercise authority over them. Yet it shall not be so among you; but whoever desires to become great among you shall be your servant. And whoever of you desires to be first shall be slave of all. For even the Son of Man did not come to be served, but to serve, and to give His life a ransom for many."'—Mark 10:35-45*

Jesus immediately dispelled the false expectation James and John had. The other disciples were right in being displeased, and Jesus could have been too. But Jesus didn't sit with the disappointment, He instead adjusted the expectation. He showed a better way. He completely turned the expectation on its head.

In another example, Peter's question indicated he had been disappointed somehow with others, although the Bible doesn't say how.

> *'Then Peter came to Him and said, "Lord, how often shall my brother sin against me, and I forgive him? Up to seven times?" Jesus said to him, "I do not say to you, up to seven times, but up to seventy times seven."'*—
> Matthew 18:21-22

Again, Jesus immediately turned the expectation upside down and spoke of a better way, God's way. The way of forgiveness, which is a crucial step towards overcoming disappointment from other people.

Finally, following the arrest of Jesus, where He was being tried and beaten, Peter denied Jesus to three different people when they asked if he knew Him. Then, at Jesus' crucifixion, Peter disappointed himself so badly when he denied knowing Jesus that he wept bitterly.

> *'And the Lord turned and looked at Peter. Then Peter remembered the word of the Lord, how He had said to him, "Before the rooster crows, you will deny Me three times." So, Peter went out and wept bitterly.'*—
> Luke 22:61-62

The way Jesus restored and forgave Peter was an incredibly beautiful moment. Following His resurrection, Jesus went to the beach and cooked His disciples' breakfast when they had come onto shore from fishing.

Jesus asked Peter three times if He loves Him, the same number of times Peter denied Him. Jesus restored Peter then proceeded to commission him into God's calling and purpose.

> *'A third time he asked him, "Simon son of John, do you love me?" Peter was hurt that Jesus asked the question a third time. He said, "Lord,*

you know everything. You know that I love you." Jesus said, "Then feed my sheep."'—John 21:17 (NLT)

Peter's process of overcoming disappointment in himself was repentance and feeling sorrow for what he had done when he wept bitterly. Then he received Jesus' forgiveness and restoration. The way he went forward into the mission God had called him to throughout Acts would suggest he had forgiven himself as well and not allowed his failure to paralyse him with disappointment.

Romans 5 tells us that God's hope will never lead to disappointment. The hope given by others or the hope we give ourselves will disappoint, but God will never disappoint us.

> *'Therefore, since we have been made right in God's sight by faith, we have peace with God because of what Jesus Christ our Lord has done for us. Because of our faith, Christ has brought us into this place of undeserved privilege where we now stand, and we confidently and joyfully look forward to sharing God's glory. We can rejoice, too, when we run into problems and trials, for we know that they help us develop endurance. And endurance develops strength of character, and character strengthens our confident hope of salvation. And this hope will not lead to disappointment. For we know how dearly God loves us, because he has given us the Holy Spirit to fill our hearts with his love... So now we can rejoice in our wonderful new relationship with God because our Lord Jesus Christ has made us friends of God.'—Romans 5:1-12 (NLT)*

Let some of those truths sink deep into your soul, into your heart, into your spirit and allow them to wash away the disappointments. We have peace with God; we have undeserved privilege, we can have a confident hope of salvation, Holy Spirit fills our hearts with God's dear love, we have a wonderful new relationship with God, and we are God's friends! All of that combined with His expectation, not our own, and His forgiveness when we fail, enable us to process and overcome the disappointments that life will bring our way.

Selah: stop, connect, enjoy ...

Let's get rid of those insidious joy busters!

Comparison

Think about the unhelpful measuring stick you may use to compare with others.

Make a list of your strengths and weaknesses.

Spend some time with God and ask Him what He uniquely wants you to do and say and be in this season. Ask Him what is His race and lane for you to run in?

Meditate on this profound passage:

> 'For You formed my inward parts; You covered me in my mother's womb. I will praise You, for I am fearfully and wonderfully made; Marvellous are Your works, and that my soul knows very well. My frame was not hidden from You, when I was made in secret, and skilfully wrought in the lowest parts of the earth. Your eyes saw my substance, being yet unformed. And in Your book they all were written, the days fashioned for me, when as yet there were none of them. How precious also are Your thoughts to me, O God! How great is the sum of them! If I should count them, they would be more in number than the sand ...'—Psalm 139:13-18

Ask God to show you what He has written in your book about the days He has fashioned for you.

Think about this statement: If we are clothed in love and are kind, gentle and patient, we will not be comparing but celebrating.

Ask yourself: do I compare or celebrate others? How can I clothe myself 'with the presence of the Lord Jesus Christ' and in 'tender-hearted mercy, kindness, humility, gentleness, patience and love'?

Do you have a good understanding of your identity as a son or daughter of God through Christ Jesus?

Meditate on these passages and ask God to speak to your identity through them:

> 'Behold what manner of love the Father has bestowed on us, that we should be called children of God!'—1 John 3:1

> 'For as many as are led by the Spirit of God, these are sons of God. For you did not receive the spirit of bondage again to fear, but you received the Spirit of adoption by whom we cry out, 'Abba, Father.' The Spirit Himself bears witness with our spirit that we are children of God, and if children, then heirs—heirs of God and joint heirs with Christ, if indeed we suffer with Him, that we may also be glorified together.'—Romans 8:14-17

If you would like to delve into this at a deeper level, read *The Supernatural Ways of Royalty: Discovering Your Rights and Privileges of Being a Son or Daughter of God* by Kris Vallotton and Bill Johnson. [68]

Consider this statement: If I am comparing, then I am essentially judging that you are either superior or inferior to me.

Ask yourself: Do I fall into the trap of judging through comparison? How can I 'judge not' so I 'won't be judged'?

Disappointment

Read the following quote again:

> 'Repeated disappointment almost always triggers a series of other reactions: discouragement, anger, frustration, bitterness, resentment, even depression. Unless we learn to deal with disappointment, it will rob us of joy and poison our souls.'[69] —Billy Graham

Have an honest talk with God and ask Him to reveal if anything in the quote above is present in your life.

Read Psalm 62. Reflect on where your expectation comes from. Ask God to adjust your expectations to line up with His.

Take some time to declutter and sort your expectations. Which expectations have to go into the trash? Which expectations are recyclable and can be re-purposed? Which expectations are to keep? Which expectations are to keep with some alterations?

Do you deep down believe God is good? Are there any other truths which, if you are honest with yourself, you do not believe in your heart? Ask God for a fresh encounter with Him. Ask Him to reveal His truth to you and renew your mind.

What might God be saying to you about turning your DIS-appointment into His appointment?

Has another person disappointed you?

Ask yourself: what are my expectations on this person and are they realistic? Spend some time in prayer with God and intentionally forgive them. Ask Him to show you the way forward for this relationship without further disappointment.

Are you disappointed with yourself?

Do you have high expectations yourself from perfectionism or performance mentality? Are your expectations on yourself so rigid that it is difficult to cope when they are not met? How can you challenge this thinking and renew your mind?

Is it possible you may be viewing some of your areas of disappointment from the wrong perspective? What is God's viewpoint?

If you are disappointed in yourself, spend some time repenting if it is from a wrongdoing. Receive Jesus' forgiveness and ask Him to show you His way of restoration. Ask God to help you forgive yourself and how to not allow your failure to paralyse you with disappointment.

Meditate on this passage and allow the truths to sink deep into your soul, into your heart, into your spirit and wash away the disappointments.

> 'Therefore, since we have been made right in God's sight by faith, we have peace with God because of what Jesus Christ our Lord has done for us. Because of our faith, Christ has brought us into this place of undeserved privilege where we now stand, and we confidently and joyfully look forward to sharing God's glory. We can rejoice, too, when we run into problems and trials, for we know that they help us develop endurance. And endurance develops strength of character, and character strengthens our confident hope of salvation. And this hope will not lead to disappointment. For we know how dearly God loves us, because he has given us the Holy Spirit to fill our hearts with his love... So now we can rejoice in our wonderful new relationship with God because our Lord Jesus Christ has made us friends of God.'—Romans 5:1-12 (NLT)

9. JOY Busters: Toxic Thinking, Un-forgiveness, & Bad Attitudes

Joy Buster 7: Toxic thinking

Have you ever asked yourself the question: how much head space am I wasting?

Neuroscientist Dr Caroline Leaf tells us that thoughts do actually occupy space in our brain.

> *'Thoughts are real, physical things that occupy mental real estate. Moment by moment, every day, you are changing the structure of your brain through your thinking.'*[70]

Toxic, distorted thinking is a waste of head space. We waste so much time thinking unhelpful, unhealthy thoughts; thoughts that bust our joy. Negativity, catastrophic thinking and lies from the enemy of our soul: these all bust our joy. Thoughts that sound like 'should', 'if-only' and 'what if', and even include dread and belittling oneself all **bust our joy**.

Not sure about you, but I want to be a good steward of the time God has given me on this earth and this includes my thought life.

When I stop and think about what I'm thinking about, sometimes I'm astounded at how much headspace and time I'm wasting thinking negative, pointless and unhelpful thoughts. I've had to stop and remind myself what a waste of headspace those thoughts are: not only does it waste mine and God's time, it also busts my joy!

In the biographical movie, *Darkest Hour*, Winston Churchill declares, 'Those who never change their minds, never change anything.'[71]

Just take a moment to think on that statement. Those who never change their minds, ***never change anything***.

Change your mind, change your life

Empirical evidence reveals this is scientifically possible. Dr Leaf's research has shown that the brain is capable of changing itself (neuroplasticity) through directed mind training.

> *'Each time a thought dominates your conscious mind, you can do something with it. You are not a victim of your biology; you can control your reactions to events and circumstances. You can choose to keep your thinking the same or change it. Either way, protein synthesis happens. The toxic memory will either be changed or strengthened.'*[72]—*Dr Caroline Leaf*

This is significant! Just because you have a pattern of thinking a certain way, and the propensity to think that way may even be in your DNA, it is possible to change.[73] The Bible also tells us this is possible: 'be transformed by the renewing of your mind.'—Romans 12:2

In fact, when we turn our lives over to Jesus, the Bible tells us we are new creations, which means we now have God's DNA. Through the enabling power and help of the Holy Spirit, we no longer have to walk according to our old ways of thinking and living.

> *'Therefore, if anyone is in Christ, he is a new creation; old things have passed away; behold, all things have become new.'*—*2 Corinthians 5:17*

> *'... be renewed in the spirit of your mind, and ... put on the new man which was created according to God, in true righteousness and holiness.'*—*Ephesians 4:23-24*

In order to re-find or find joy, something has to change and that 'something' usually has a thought behind it. In order to bring about personal change, it will most likely require changing your thinking.

What we think is who we are

The Bible tells us we become, and act on, what we are thinking about.

'For as he thinks in his heart, so is he.'
—Proverbs 23:7

'... out of the abundance of the heart the mouth speaks.'
—Matthew 12:24

It follows then: what we sow into our heart is what will come out. What we give head space to is what we will be. The Apostle Paul gives us some help about what is beneficial to be thinking about.

'And now, dear brothers and sisters, one final thing. Fix your thoughts on what is true, and honourable, and right, and pure, and lovely, and admirable. Think about things that are excellent and worthy of praise. Keep putting into practice all you learned and received from me— everything you heard from me and saw me doing. Then the God of peace will be with you.'—Philippians 4:8-9 (NLT)

When he wrote this letter to the church in Philippi, he was writing from a decrepit, miserable Roman prison. It wasn't like he was sitting at a beautiful garden bench in a garden of roses at the time. He wasn't even in a 21st century prison with modern-day improvements. Roman prisons were filthy, cold, and dark with a vile stench. It is thought Paul was in the Tullianum room in the Mamertine prison. This room was located in a sewer system below the city![74]

You may remember the old saying: 'There are two men in prison. One sees the bars, the other one sees the stars.' Well the apostle Paul took it a step further and saw the One who made the stars!

Let's look at the **opposite** to our passage from Philippians.

Fix your thoughts on what is false, and dishonourable, and wrong, and impure, and unpleasant, and despicable. Think about things that are pathetic and unworthy of praise.

It almost busts your joy just reading them!

How can we fix and adjust our thoughts? By knowing what the Word of God says so we can think on the truth. By asking Holy Spirit to empower and enable us to think better and transform us by the renewing of our mind and by ruling our thoughts and by shutting the door on wrong thoughts.

What's behind the door?

You may have seen the old movie *Sliding Doors*.[75] In the movie, the character goes through one door into one life-path. The movie then shows what happens if she didn't go through that door. Her life turned out completely different depending on which door she went through.

What if we could shut the door on the wrong thoughts and open the door to true, honourable, right, pure, lovely, admirable, excellent, and praiseworthy thoughts? It could fundamentally shape who we are and the decisions and outcomes in our life. Depending on which door we allow our thoughts to go through could shape our life completely differently. At the very least, it will shape our joy and peace.

Example: fear and worry, 'what if' thinking.

Door 1 Thinking: You might think along these lines: 'What if ... they don't like me? I start the new job and can't do it? I don't have enough money or talent or skill or I don't know what to say? What if someone I love has a freak accident and dies? What if I get sick and die young?'

Door 2 Thinking: Make a change in your thinking such as, 'No, stop it! That is fear, it is not true. I will cross that bridge when or *if* it comes, but there is no point worrying about something that may never happen. Jesus said not to worry about tomorrow, and He said to be anxious for nothing. So I will talk to Him about it and 'cast it' on Him, reminding myself to cast all my care upon Him, for He cares for me (1 Peter 5:7).'

It might look like this as a prayer:

> *'Lord, I hand my worries (name them) to You and ask you to direct me back to You as each new worry arises. Help me work through my problems one step at a time. I choose to believe Your good report, the Word of God. I choose to be grateful and I'm going to fill my head space with Your peace and joy.'*

Outcome of Door 1: A head full of fear and worry. Loss of sleep, loss of confidence, loss of hope, loss of peace, loss of joy.

Outcome of Door 2: You will most likely have a better night's sleep. You won't be wasting head space on unnecessary 'what if's' that may never happen. You will increase the ability to think more productively and solve problems in a rational head space full of God's peace and joy.

We all have habitual patterns of thinking. It is well known that it can take approximately 21 days to form a habit, so we will need to shut a lot of doors on those thoughts that are patterns in our life and probably do it more than once.

Next time you find yourself with toxic, out-of-control thoughts which are opposite to healthy, helpful thinking, try instructing yourself: 'that's a waste of head space'. And then shut the door on that thought. Open the door to Holy Spirit led thinking, and meditate on 'Whatever is true, noble, just, pure, lovely, of good report, of virtue and praise-worthy.'—Philippians 4:8-9 (NKJV)

I encourage you to take up a personal mission to rule your thoughts rather than let them rule you. If you would like to delve deeper into this, I recommend reading *Who Switched Off My Brain? Controlling Toxic Thoughts and Emotions* by Dr Caroline Leaf.[76]

She also has an app called SWITCH which uses her scientifically researched and revolutionary SWITCH on Your Brain 5 Step Process® to help you take back control over your thoughts and your life.[77] I can personally attest to the effectiveness of this app in my life. It even affected my physical health when I got my thoughts under control through this process.

Joy Buster 8: Unforgiveness

'Unforgiveness is like drinking poison yourself and waiting for the other person to die.'—Marianne Williamson[78]

The poison of unforgiveness is a definite joy buster. It will consume you until there is no room for any joy. Unforgiveness will have you tied up in knots whenever the other person's name is mentioned or when a memory pops up from your time with that person. Unforgiveness will keep you focussed on the pain and yield a victim mentality and inevitably lead to bitterness.

> *'As I walked out the door toward the gate that would lead to my freedom, I knew if I didn't leave my bitterness and hatred behind, I'd still be in prison.'*[79]*—Nelson Mandela*

Let's use the same 'sliding door' concept again to see how unforgiveness can rob us of joy.

Example: Someone says or does something which hurts us which, of course, happens to all of us.

Door 1 Thinking: You might think along these lines: 'How dare they, it's unforgivable, it's not fair, maybe there's something wrong with me to be treated like this, I'm going to give them what they deserve.'

You then proceed to prepare a whole courtroom defence in your mind about how a conversation you'll probably never have, nor should have, plays out. In this scene, you are defending yourself and proving why they are wrong, and you are right. In your mind, it sounds just and reasonable. Can you relate?

Door 2 Thinking: Make a change in your thinking such as, 'That really hurt, and it's not fair. Hurt people, hurt people, so they must be feeling pretty awful to go out of their way to upset me like this. I wonder if there is a misunderstanding that we can sort out? What is within my power to do as the Bible says, to make it my aim to be at peace with everyone? Is it possible there is some way I can go to them to reconcile, or is it better not to? What is the right thing to do, even if they were wrong? How can I think well of them in spite of all this?'

It might look like this as a prayer:

> *'Lord, you know that this situation has really hurt me. I give you the pain that I feel and ask that you show me what is within my power to do as the Bible says, to make it my aim to be at peace with this person. Show me if it's better to try and reconcile or not to? Show me what is the right thing to do even if they were wrong and how I can think well of them in spite of all this.*

Then, instead of the courtroom drama, the scene plays out like this. "Well, I am so forgiven by God and He loves me, and He said I am to forgive others, so He can forgive me, so I will make a conscious choice to forgive and let the feelings catch up later."

> *'If you forgive those who sin against you, your heavenly Father will forgive you. But if you refuse to forgive others, your Father will not forgive your sins.'*—Matthew 6:14-15 (NLT)

I will allow God's love and what He says about me to dictate what I believe about myself; not what people may say. I will pray for them as Jesus has asked me to: 'Love your enemies! Pray for those who persecute you!'—Matthew 5:44 (NLT)

Outcome of Door 1: Bitter and bound up in un-forgiveness. God's mercy and forgiveness are even limited when I don't forgive others. There is little chance of reconciliation and it can only come from them. Troubled and consuming thoughts with no peace or joy.

Outcome of Door 2: Peace of mind and free from bitterness. There is a possibility of reconciliation. Less wasted head space and peace with God. The opening of the door to joy even in the situation.

Un-forgiveness opens the door to bitterness. I must confess I carried some bitterness in my heart during that 'loss of joy' season. Bitterness is ugly and not at all pleasant, definitely something to avoid.

> *'Work at living in peace with everyone ... Look after each other so that none of you fails to receive the grace of God. Watch out that no poisonous root of bitterness grows up to trouble you, corrupting many.'*—Hebrews 12:14-15 (NLT)

Bitterness: a troubling poisonous root

Have you ever grown mint? We have an herb garden and when I was weeding it recently, I found the mint roots had grown everywhere through the whole garden. Not that mint is poisonous or bitter, far from it, however its roots do the same as bitterness. Its roots affect the root systems of all the other plants around it and it can be found springing up all over the garden community.

Likewise, in a human community, a root of bitterness can affect all in the community. It can spread and spring up all over the community like a poison.

What Jesus has to say about un-forgiveness is rather confronting. I know I definitely need and want the forgiveness of Father God in my life. Does He actually say that He will not forgive us if we don't forgive others? Yes, in two eyewitness accounts; in Matthew, as above, and in Mark.

> *'And whenever you stand praying, if you have anything against anyone, forgive him, that your Father in heaven may also forgive you your trespasses. But if you do not forgive, neither will your Father in heaven forgive your trespasses.'*—Mark 11: 25-26

That is a rather weighty statement! We know God is the source of joy, and there is fullness of joy in His Presence. If un-forgiveness affronts our relationship with the source, then joy will most definitely be lacking.

Forgiveness does not downplay the pain

What Jesus is not saying is to allow them to continue to hurt you. If you are in an abusive situation, withdrawing from that situation is not un-forgiveness, it is wisdom. When you are removed from the situation, then He asks you to make the choice to forgive them. That does not mean you have to even see them again. We can forgive them in a place of prayer just between you and God, or if you are struggling to do this, go through the forgiveness process with a trusted friend. Hand them over to God and decide to forgive them. You won't feel like forgiving, but when you make the decision then the pain will gradually fade. If it is a deep hurt, the process will take some time, not necessarily an overnight quick fix. This can be painful. However, if you don't forgive, if you don't engage in the process of forgiving, the pain will increase as you play it over and over in your head and it becomes consuming.

The process of forgiveness involves naming the pain, and the wrong done. You have to know what you are forgiving them for. If you say how you were wronged out loud (even just between you and God), then you can say out loud that you forgive that wrong and that pain. Jesus also calls us to pray for those who have hurt us (Matthew 5:44 quoted above). When we pray for someone, it will always bring about the right heart in us toward them.

Sometimes God will ask you to process the forgiveness with the person or to write a letter to the person. Sometimes it will be just between you and God. Ask God which way to go about this and proceed according to what He gives you peace about. He always knows best, and He knows the other side of this process. He knows if it is a matter of reconciliation or a matter of letting go.

The enemy of our souls, the devil, is always about division and discord. In fact, that is how he came about being the devil. He was an angel in heaven and stirred up dissension against God and His other angels.

> 'Then there was war in heaven. Michael and his angels fought against the dragon and his angels. And the dragon lost the battle, and he and his angels were forced out of heaven. This great dragon—the ancient serpent called the devil, or Satan, the one deceiving the whole world—was thrown down to the earth with all his angels. Then I heard a loud voice shouting across the heavens, 'It has come at last—salvation and power and the Kingdom of our God, and the authority of his Christ. For the accuser of our brothers and sisters has been thrown down to earth—the one who accuses them before our

God day and night. And they have defeated him by the blood of the Lamb and by their testimony."—Revelation 12:7-11 (NLT)

Satan does not like the fact that he is defeated, so he will stir up any trouble possible. If he can cause 'war' between the people God created and loves, he will. If there is confusion between you and others, you can be sure it's not God but the enemy trying to disrupt harmony and peace.

'For God is not the author of confusion but of peace.'
—1 Corinthians 14:33

Sometimes you can sense confusion when it feels like you are communicating from different planets. That is the time to stop and sort out any misunderstanding. With small differences, it is often a misunderstanding, whereby you are hearing differently to what the person is saying and misjudging their heart behind it.

Whether it is a minor matter or a deeply painful experience, make the decision to forgive and not allow un-forgiveness to poison your soul and rob your joy.

Joy Buster 9: Bad Attitudes

'Watch out for the joy-stealers: gossip, criticism, complaining, fault-finding, and a negative, judgmental attitude.'[80] —Joyce Meyer

I tried to have a 'bad attitude', I gave it a go, and it does not provide the fun, relief, and joy it promises.

Some of the bad attitudes I've engaged in have involved whinging, criticism, negativity, defiance and self-focus. None of them brought any joy; quite the contrary. They only brought darkness instead of light. They produced a sour 'taste' in my heart.

At one point I remember deciding that a good attitude clearly wasn't working because of the difficult circumstances. What I discovered was that a bad attitude didn't change the circumstances; it just made them more difficult to endure without the accompanying peace and joy of the Lord.

Thinking about it logically, let's look at the attitudes mentioned above.

Gossip: this attitude usually stems from a poor self-image and an attempt to make one-self look better by putting others down. Logically, it actually makes one-self look petty and insecure by the need to speak ill of others.

Criticism and fault-finding: in a similar vein to gossip, tearing down may seem like a path to building one-self up. There is a difference between constructive criticism that aims to bring out the best and encourage, and a critical spirit which will go looking for fuel to belittle and nit-pick. Fault-finding, for the sake of it, will only cast a negative spin on anything and everything and leave a wake of joylessness.

Complaining: well this is completely fruitless. Complaining only makes you go around in circles like God's people in the Old Testament. They took forty years to make an eleven-day journey because of their complaining and bad attitude (see Deuteronomy 1:2, Numbers 11, 14 and 16).

Complaining about something will not change it. The advantage of complaining is the indulgence that comes with self-pity. I used to be quite good at pity parties. At these parties, there was plenty of whining, excuse the pun, and looking at the green grass on the other side. None of these activities are worthwhile in the aim to eliminate the problems. If anything, they compound the issues by giving them more focus time than they need.

Negative, judgmental attitude: There is no joy in negativity. Yes, we need to be authentic and not unrealistically optimistic. However, gratitude and looking for the good keeps us in a good head space; always searching for the worst and looking for what we can see is wrong as the priority dampens and disheartens. Being overly judgmental is a repellent. People do not generally like to feel judged, and this attitude drives people away.

Defiance and self-focus: Joy is sown into our heart by God when we are upright in heart. Through Jesus Christ, our spiritual standing is holy before God. To walk this out practically, we yield our hearts to God and lean into receiving His love, power, guidance, conviction, and instructions. When our heart is yielded to God, the source of joy, He is able to release joy into our hearts. But if we want to go our own way, He allows that, including the consequences.

> *'Light is sown for the [uncompromisingly] righteous and strewn along their pathway, and joy for the upright in heart [the irrepressible joy which comes from consciousness of His favour and protection].'*—Psalm 97:11 (AMPC)

My conclusion, having tried both bad and good attitude? I recommend choosing a good, surrendered to God attitude every time.

Find freedom

This brings us to the conclusion of the joy busters. Joy busters are prevented in two ways. Some are simply making a decision to avoid them. Others are changed by discovering the root cause of why we allow that joy buster in our life.

At the root is where transformation is actualised at a deep level by the power of Holy Spirit. This is where we discover and disagree with lies we may have believed. This is where Jesus can release healing and transformation, and where we can seek God for revelation and insight into the unhelpful patterns in our life.

Sometimes the root cause is found by asking God to reveal it to us. When there is no breakthrough, it is wise to reach out and ask a trusted Christian leader or counsellor to pray for you and work it through with you.

My prayer for you is that Holy Spirit would be gently prodding you as you have read these past three chapters and revealing the joy busters in your life. When He does, spend some time praying and asking Jesus to set you free.

'So, we praise God for the glorious grace he has poured out on us who belong to his dear Son. He is so rich in kindness and grace that he purchased our freedom with the blood of his Son and forgave our sins. He has showered his kindness on us, along with all wisdom and understanding.'—Ephesians 1:6-8 (NLT)

Selah: stop, connect, enjoy ...

It's time for an attitude check.

Ask yourself the question: how much head space am I wasting? What are the thoughts that are wasting my head space?

How can you shut the door on those thoughts and go through the door of healthy thinking in that area?

Are any of the following types of thinking busting my joy?

- Negativity
- Catastrophic thinking
- Lies from the enemy of our soul
- Thoughts that sound like 'should', 'if-only' and 'what if'
- Thoughts that include dread and belittling oneself

Are any of the following types of bad attitudes busting my joy?

- Gossip
- Criticism and fault-finding
- Complaining
- Negative and judgmental
- Defiance and self-focus

Ponder on how you can change your thoughts using Philippians 4:8-9 (NLT) as your template:

> 'Fix your thoughts on what is **true**, *and* **honourable**, *and* **right**, *and* **pure**, *and* **lovely**, *and* **admirable**. *Think about things that are* **excellent** *and* **worthy of praise**.'

Ask yourself: Am I harbouring unforgiveness or bitterness in my heart?

Spend some time with God praying and forgiving those who have wronged you. Ask God if there is any further action you need to take such as writing to them or contacting them. If it is a particularly deep issue and the pain is unbearable, consider seeking help from a pastor or counsellor to process the pain and come to a place of forgiveness.

Perhaps you are bitter towards God? God's ways are always perfect but sometimes things happen which may cause you to question that. Meditate on the following passage and ask God to reveal His character, love, and goodness to you.

> *'As for God, His way is perfect; the word of the Lord is proven; He is a shield to all who trust in Him. For who is God, except the Lord? And who is a rock, except our God? It is God who arms me with strength...'—Psalm 18:30-32*

Give yourself an attitude check-up. Ask Holy Spirit to reveal any attitudes which are not helpful.

Ask God to reveal to you the root cause of the joy busters in your life. Pray for freedom in the name of Jesus Christ.

> *'So, we praise God for the glorious grace he has poured out on us who belong to his dear Son. He is so rich in kindness and grace that he purchased our freedom with the blood of his Son and forgave our sins. He has showered his kindness on us, along with all wisdom and understanding.'—Ephesians 1:6-8 (NLT)*

10. Joy Inexpressible

'All praise to God, the Father of our Lord Jesus Christ. It is by his great mercy that we have been born again because God raised Jesus Christ from the dead. Now we live with great expectation, and we have a priceless inheritance—an inheritance that is kept in heaven for you, pure and undefiled, beyond the reach of change and decay. And through your faith, God is protecting you by his power until you receive this salvation, which is ready to be revealed on the last day for all to see.

So be truly glad. There is wonderful joy ahead, even though you must endure many trials for a little while. These trials will show that your faith is genuine. It is being tested as fire tests and purifies gold—though your faith is far more precious than mere gold. So, when your faith remains strong through many trials, it will bring you much praise and glory and honour on the day when Jesus Christ is revealed to the whole world. You love Him even though you have never seen Him. Though you do not see him now, you trust him; and you rejoice with a glorious, inexpressible joy.'—1 Peter 1:3-12 (NLT)

Joy inexpressible! That is God's promise to us! It means joy so deep that you can't even describe it; indescribable; beyond understanding; indefinable; unspeakable! Peter is saying: 'I wish I could describe it to you, but I can't'.

Looking at this passage, how do we experience joy inexpressible?

It is through 'grace recognised'. It is by having deep heart revelation of God's great mercy and the priceless inheritance we have through Jesus Christ our Lord and living with great expectation in God's—not our own—expectations. It is through faith; through deciding to be truly glad and through seeing our trials as an opportunity for gold to be formed in us. It is by loving and trusting Jesus with all our hearts and minds and rejoicing because of all the above.

> *'There is a joy which is not given to the ungodly, but to those who love Thee for Thine own sake, whose joy Thou Thyself art. And this is the happy life, to rejoice to Thee, of Thee, for Thee; this is it, and there is no other.'*—Augustine

This joy is found in the person of Jesus and in the place of knowing Him; of loving Jesus and of trusting Him. As 1 Peter 1:12 says, this inexpressible joy comes to those who love Jesus by faith, without seeing Him. This is the kind of faith that knows that Jesus is who He says He is and will do what He says He will do. It is a deep conviction that the Word of God, the Bible, is categorical truth and God's Words are absolutely words to live by.

As we come to the last chapter of this book, I would like to share with you one of my prayers I pray from time to time.

I like to pray that God would make me like a sparkling oak tree. During the year of my 'finding joy' journey, we had dinner at a beautiful old pub near our church in Sydney called The Oaks. There are several magnificent old oak trees in the courtyard which are decorated with fairy lights. Looking up through the branches, it was so exquisite. The trees have immense, ancient trunks with expansive branches spreading out as a covering above the dining tables. The lights sparkle against the green of the oak leaves and create a magical canopy.

During that period, I repeatedly asked God to make me sparkle for Jesus. I wanted to have a faith and joy that is contagious. I did not wish for my lack of joy to prevent others from knowing the inexpressible joy that can be found in Jesus. The next time I prayed this, the oak tree sparkling lights canopy came to mind. I sensed God was saying to me to pray that I'd not only sparkle but be like an oak tree as well; a sparkling oak tree.

> *'The Spirit of the Lord God is upon me ... to grant [consolation and joy] to those who mourn in Zion—to give them an ornament (a garland or diadem) of beauty instead of ashes, the oil of joy instead of mourning, the garment [expressive] of praise instead of a heavy, burdened, and failing spirit—that they may be called oaks of righteousness [lofty,*

> *strong, and magnificent, distinguished for uprightness, justice, and right standing with God], the planting of the Lord, that He may be glorified.'—Isaiah 61:1,3 (AMPC)*

When the Spirit of the Lord is on us, we are planted by the Lord to bring Him glory, similar to the robust, unwavering, and deep-rooted oak tree. The Spirit of the Lord anoints us to release the oil of the joy of the Lord wherever we go. When we are full of His joy, it overflows. When we have our internal 'sparkle' resulting from being full of His joy, we will be overflowing vessels of His joy with the deep-rooted stability of being planted in Him.

Worship

No book about joy would be complete without giving an enormous shout out to the significance of worship. Our passage for this chapter in 1 Peter starts with an exclamation of worship, giving all praise to God.

The Biblical Greek word for worship is '*proskuneo*', which means to kiss (towards) one, in token of reverence ... to fall upon the knees and touch the ground with the forehead as an expression of profound reverence ... kneeling or prostration to do homage (to one) or make obeisance, whether in order to express respect or to make supplication.[81]

The most popular modern form of worship is through music and the profound lyrics that have been put to it. These lyrics magnify God and kiss towards Him. Worship songs express reverence and homage to the King of Kings and Lord of Lords; the Creator of the Universe; the Lover of our souls; the Holy Almighty God!

If poetry is more your style, worship can be expressed through poems. Some find art and dance a creative expression of giving homage to God. Some find meditating on who God is, His goodness and all His various character traits, as a powerful form of worship. Whatever your preferred style may be, the focus here is kissing towards Him, expressing respect for Him, and showing reverence to Him.

When we 'recognise His grace' and our heart is filled with joy because of who He is, we burst out in worship, just as the Psalmist did.

> 'The Lord is my strength and shield. I trust him with all my heart. He helps me, and my heart is filled with joy. I burst out in songs of thanksgiving.'—Psalm 28:7 (NLT)

We said earlier that Corrie ten Boom had said: 'Worry is a cycle of inefficient thoughts whirling around a centre of fear.'

Similarly, worship is a cycle of efficient thoughts where Jesus is at the centre.

When I recognise and receive God's love and grace towards me, I want to worship Him. When I worship Him, I recognise more of His amazing love and grace, which produces a desire to worship Him more. Then I recognise more of His love and grace. And so on. Through this cycle comes that deep joy that transcends circumstances, emotions, and negative thinking.

The Bible speaks of worship as magnifying God.

> 'I will praise the name of God with a song and will magnify Him with thanksgiving.'—Psalm 69:30

> 'When Jesus had spoken these things, He lifted up His eyes to heaven and said, Father, the hour has come. Glorify and exalt and honour and magnify Your Son, so that Your Son may glorify and extol and honour and magnify You.'—John 17:1

Worship magnifies God and minimises everything else

If we are magnifying God, it forces our problems to diminish in the light of His glory and grace. This gives room for joy and peace, as the beautiful old hymn says:

> *'Turn your eyes upon Jesus,*
> *Look full in His wonderful face,*
> *And the things of earth will grow strangely dim,*
> *In the light of His glory and grace.'*
> *- Public Domain*

The devil, the enemy of our souls, can hear us as we extol the goodness of God and declare the victory that is found in Jesus Christ. He knows he is defeated, and our act of worship pushes back darkness. As we proclaim the truth of God and who He is, lies are dispelled from our thinking. As we worship, we magnify Jesus as our Victor; our Defender; our Redeemer; our King; our Lord. As we magnify Jesus, the enemy's effect is defeated in our lives. As we worship, Holy Spirit pours His love into our hearts and we receive a deep revelation of the love of God; assurance that God is with us and for us; and a deep heart 'knowing' of God's faithfulness and goodness. As we worship, the joy of the Lord becomes our strength. Here's a good prayer found right in scripture:

> *'Satisfy us each morning with your unfailing love, so we may sing for joy to the end of our lives.'* —Psalm 90:14 (NLT)

There is a beautiful song by Bethel Music 'Love Has a Name' and the lyrics ascribe joy to the name of Jesus. 'Joy has a name: Jesus'!

> *'There's a joy that triumphs over fear,*
> *There's a laughter that wipes away all tears,*
> *There's a presence that changes atmospheres,*
> *There's a name.*
> *We will fix our eyes on the One who overcame,*
> *We will stand in awe of the One who breaks the chains.*
> *Love has a name, Jesus!*
> *Victory has a name, Jesus!*
> *Joy has a name, Joy has a name, JESUS!'*[82]

It's all about Jesus

The Bible tells us there is power in the name of Jesus, the name above every other name.
God also has highly exalted Him and given Him the name which is above every name, that at the name of Jesus every knee should bow, of those in heaven, and of those on earth, and of those under the earth, and that every tongue should confess that Jesus Christ is Lord, to the glory of God the Father.'—Philippians 2:9-11

> 'Most assuredly, I say to you, whatever you ask the Father in My name He will give you. Until now you have asked nothing in My name. Ask, and you will receive, that your joy may be full.'—John 16:23-24

When we confess Jesus is Lord and pray in His name, according to His will, joy is released in our spirit. During my 'joy journey' season, when I understood that praise and thankfulness releases joy, sometimes I would just declare 'Hallelujah, thank you Jesus'. And this released joy into my soul and my spirit.

Sometimes when we are weary, we don't have many words, but I found these summed it all up. Not because those words are somehow magical, rather it is because I declared them with meaning. Hallelujah means: *halela-yah, 'praise ye Yah'*[83]. So, when we say 'hallelujah' with our faith and trust behind it, we give God praise for who He is. When I discovered that thankfulness is crucial to release joy, I would say 'thank you Jesus' out of gratefulness for all He has done for me and for His unfailing love and amazing grace: 'grace recognised'.

The joy of the Lord is my strength

Probably the most commonly quoted verse on joy in the Bible is found in Nehemiah 8:10.

Let me explain some context. God's people had been in exile and God raised up Nehemiah to lead the people into rebuilding the walls of their city, Jerusalem. Through much opposition, they rebuilt the walls and acknowledged it was due to God's help (Nehemiah 6:16). Nehemiah called them to gather in the public square. They asked Ezra, the priest and scribe, to read God's Words to them. When they heard the Words of God read to them, they all broke down and wept when they realised they had strayed so far from them.

Then Nehemiah told them not to weep because of their sin but instead to proclaim the goodness of the Lord; to celebrate that they now knew His Words and understood how to live going forward. Nehemiah declared to the people that the joy of the Lord is their strength.

> *'Then Nehemiah the governor, Ezra the priest and scribe, and the Levites who were interpreting for the people said to them, 'Don't mourn or weep on such a day as this! For today is a sacred day before the Lord your God.' For the people had all been weeping as they listened to the words of the Law. And Nehemiah continued, 'Go and celebrate with a feast of rich foods and sweet drinks and share gifts of food with people who have nothing prepared. This is a sacred day before our Lord. Don't be dejected and sad, for **the joy of the Lord is your strength!**"And the Levites, too, quieted the people, telling them, 'Hush! Don't weep! For this is a sacred day.' So, the people went away to eat and drink at a festive meal, to share gifts of food, and to celebrate with great joy because they had heard God's words and understood them.'*—Nehemiah 8:9-11 (NLT, emphasis added)

> In the same way, we can receive strength for our inner beings through recognising God's grace, love, and mercy towards us.

Later on, it came time to dedicate the new walls, and once again they had great joy because of what God had done for them: 'grace recognised'.

> *'Many sacrifices were offered on that joyous day, for God had given the people cause for great joy. The women and children also participated in the celebration, and the joy of the people of Jerusalem could be heard far away.'*—Nehemiah 12:43 (NLT)

We can receive strength in our souls when we understand the hope and expectation we have through the redemption of Jesus. We can receive strength when we have an ongoing and increasing comprehension of the glorious inheritance we have by faith in Christ Jesus. The joy inexpressible in the Lord and all we have in Him becomes our strength.

Prayer and Meditation

> *'When joy and prayer are married, their first-born child is gratitude.'—Charles Spurgeon*

What an incredible privilege prayer is! It is such an absolute opportunity to be able to have a dialogue with the Mighty God who created the vast universe—to have access to the presence of a Holy God. And furthermore, in His presence there is fullness of joy! (Psalm 16)

Meditation is often spoken about as a way to experience joy and happiness. Eastern meditation is emptying your mind, soul, and spirit. How much greater joy can come from having your mind, soul and spirit filled with the presence of God!

Christian meditation is filling your spirit with the very presence of God through His Holy Spirit inhabiting your spirit! It involves filling your mind and soul with the very words of the all-powerful, all-wise, all-knowing God of the universe!

> *'And I will pray the Father, and He will give you another Helper, that He may abide with you forever—the Spirit of truth, whom the world cannot receive, because it neither sees Him nor knows Him; but you know Him, for He dwells with you and will be in you. I will not leave you orphans; I will come to you. A little while longer and the world will see Me no more, but you will see Me. Because I live, you will live also. At that day you will know that I am in My Father, and you in Me, and I in you. He who has My commandments and keeps them, it is he who loves Me. And he who loves Me will be loved by My Father, and I will love him and manifest Myself to him.'—John 14:16-21*

> *'If anyone loves Me, he will keep My word; and My Father will love him, and We will come to him and make Our home with him.'—John 14:23*

The hiding place

There is a continual invitation from heaven to enter into the presence of God and be at home there. In His presence we can spend time thanking Him, talking with Him, making requests to Him and hearing from Him. The presence of God is a place of rest and of peace. His presence is like a hiding place and a place of protection for our inner being. In His hiding place and presence, He releases peace, joy, and victory.

> *'For you are my hiding place; you protect me from trouble. You surround me with songs of victory.'—Psalm 32:7 (NLT)*

I like to put on some worship music when I spend time with God and take some time to thank Him and meditate on the qualities of His awe-inspiring character. I like to ask Him questions and wait for Him to answer me through His Word, the Bible, and His quiet voice or peace in my spirit or through a picture He shows me.

God also invites us to know Him personally through studying and meditating on His Word, the Bible. When we read the Bible and ask for His Spirit to give us revelation and insight, there is boundless opportunity to be powerfully impacted and transformed and set free. Countless times, I have been reading the Bible and a verse kind of 'jumped out of the pages' at me to provide answers and guidance and freedom and conviction and insight into knowing God at a deeper heart level. The Bible truly is living and powerful and active.

The power of speaking in heavenly tongues

I believe, and have experienced, that praying in tongues releases the joy of the Lord into my spirit. This is a gift given by the Holy Spirit, which we can ask for any time after we have accepted Jesus into our hearts as our Lord and Saviour. (Acts 2:1-4)

The Bible talks about the gift of tongues whereby a word is released in a public setting and an interpretation is required. It also talks about praying and building ourselves up in our faith through speaking in tongues in our prayer time with God. Both can release joy, one into a public context and the other in our private context. (You can research this further in 1 Corinthians 14 and Jude 1:20.)

> *'For he who speaks in a tongue does not speak to men but to God, for no one understands him; however, in the spirit he speaks mysteries.'—1 Corinthians 14:2 (NLT)*

The mysteries of God release joy in our spirit when we speak in tongues as we spend time with God.

Scientists did an interesting brain study on praying in tongues:

> *'Researchers at the University of Pennsylvania took brain images of five women while they spoke in tongues and found that their frontal lobes—the thinking, wilful part of the brain through which people control what they do—were relatively quiet, as were the language centres. The regions involved in maintaining self-consciousness were active. The women were not in blind trances, and it was unclear which region was driving the behaviour ...*
>
> *Contrary to what may be a common perception, studies suggest that people who speak in tongues rarely suffer from mental problems. A recent study of nearly 1,000 evangelical Christians in England found that those who engaged in the practice were more emotionally stable than those who did not ...*
>
> *The new findings contrasted sharply with images taken of other spiritually inspired mental states like meditation, which is often a highly focused mental exercise, activating the frontal lobes .... The scans also showed a dip in the activity of a region called the left caudate. The findings from the frontal lobes are very clear, and make sense, but the caudate is usually active when you have positive affect, pleasure, positive emotions'* [84]

Let's get those 'caudates' activated! These findings line up with my experience. Sometimes I even find praying in tongues gives me actual physical energy when I'm weary. And if I'm feeling negative and downcast, praying in tongues is an incredible spiritual practice to engage in which builds up my faith, hope, peace, and joy. We access this free gift by asking God to fill us with His Spirit. Ask Him to grant you this joy of 'speaking mysteries'.

> *Father God, thank you that I am your child and have received your free gift of redemption through Jesus Christ. Thank you for your promise that you give good gifts and Your Spirit to those who ask.*
>
> *I ask You now that you would fill me with your Holy Spirit and give me the ability to speak in tongues so that I may speak to You in Your mysteries. Amen.*
>
> *(Prayer based on Luke 11:13, Acts 2:4, 1 Corinthians 14:2)*

Righteousness, peace, and joy

> *'[After all] the kingdom of God is not a matter of [getting the] food and drink [one likes], but instead it is righteousness (that state which makes a person acceptable to God) and [heart] peace and joy in the Holy Spirit.'—Romans 14:17 (AMPC)*

Righteousness, peace, and joy are all ingredients in the Kingdom of God, released by the Holy Spirit. The Kingdom of God is when His rule and reign is present in our lives.

Our righteousness is found in Christ Jesus; we are righteous before God because of His sacrifice on the cross. When we have a deep heart knowledge of this, it produces gratitude and a desire to please God because of all He has done in redeeming our lives. When we wish to please Him, we walk in line with His Spirit and in that place we are empowered for righteousness; in that place peace and joy is released in us.

If we try to be righteous in our own strength without Holy Spirit, not only does this rob our joy, but it also produces 'self-righteousness' and an internal conflict. The great apostle Paul in the Bible experienced this himself:

> *'... I want to do what is right, but I don't do it. Instead, I do what I hate ... and I know that nothing good lives in me, that is, in my sinful*

nature. I want to do what is right, but I can't. I want to do what is good, but I don't. I don't want to do what is wrong, but I do it anyway ... I have discovered this principle of life—that when I want to do what is right, I inevitably do what is wrong ... But you are not controlled by your sinful nature. You are controlled by the Spirit if you have the Spirit of God living in you ... For all who are led by the Spirit of God are children of God.'—Romans 7:15-21, 8-9, 14 (NLT)

So, joy is released when we are at peace, and peace is present when we know we are right with God and when we are led by the Spirit of God into His way of living. As children of our perfect and loving Father God, we have access to be led by His Spirit. When we are led by His Spirit, we have life, peace, and joy.

Physically and practically speaking

Most of this book has spoken into the soul/heart/spirit component of our being. Before I end this book, it would be amiss of me not to mention how vital it is to look after our bodies as a contributor to our 'joy well-being'.

God created us as whole beings: body, soul, or heart (mind, will, emotions) and spirit (where His Holy Spirit inhabits when we invite Him in). Every component affects the other components.

I was raised by two naturopathic and osteopathic parents, hence I know that what we put into our body definitely affects our health at every level. My parents recounted to me numerous stories of how changing their client's diet and nutritional intake, transformed their health physically as well as mentally.

Sometimes it's hard to change your diet, but we can all make a start by cutting back on sugar, refined flour, and processed foods, artificial colourings, and preservatives.

Here are just a few benefits from the daily practice of walking or some form of exercise:

When you go for a walk, it's not just your body that benefits, the way you think and feel changes too. The world can look better and brighter... So, how does walking bring happiness? ...

Walking sets off several processes:

- promoting the release of endorphins—'happy' hormones
- releasing adrenaline—the body's own 'mood-lifting' chemical
- producing hormones to improve sleep
- releasing muscle tension.[85]

There is a plethora of information about how to look after your body in order to affect your mental and emotional health.[86] Some other ideas to help preserve your joy and well-being:

- **Get out into God's spectacular creation and focus in on the beauty.** Command your stressful thoughts to stop and allow yourself to be in awe of God's creativity through the canvas of the earth He created. Express your praise and gratitude to Him.

    'You are worthy, O Lord, to receive glory and honour and power; for You created all things, and by Your will they exist and were created.'
    —Revelation 4:11

- **Laugh:** have a good belly laugh.

- **De-clutter:** Marie Kondo[87] has a Netflix show about de-cluttering and says to only keep that which sparks joy. We have moved house quite often. In my earlier years, I moved everything. When my parents moved into dementia care, I had to clean out their house with 25 years of clutter. This showed me the futility of keeping things. About a month later, the house we lived in sold and we also had to move. That move, I decided to de-clutter well. Surprisingly, it almost felt like I'd de-cluttered my mind and life as well.

- **Do something creative**; get those creative juices flowing! Some examples are painting, sewing, dancing, playing or listening to music, singing, craft, writing, poetry, sketching, flower arranging, gardening, baking, creating a meal, journaling, photography, scrapbooking, making cards, origami, cross-stitching, bonsai pruning, producing a movie, starting a YouTube channel, knitting, crocheting, stencilling, painting/patching clothes, renovating, etc.

- **Find your 'thing' where you feel peace and joy.** Mine is the beach. Our Melbourne COVID-19 restrictions were recently relaxed a little. As of writing this chapter, we are allowed to travel a 25km radius from our home instead of just 5km. I was beyond excited to find the beach was within our 25km. After work, we picked up burgers and went and sat and then walked on the beach. When we walked through the path onto the beach and saw and heard the waves lapping, it almost felt like my soul was being massaged. What is your 'thing' that refreshes you?

Remind me again: Why does joy matter?

I started this book with the why: why it is crucial to find your joy or get it back? Allow me to end the book by reminding you of the why.

It's not only to make you feel good, although that is an extra blessing.

1. **Joy is an essential part of being a Christ follower.** If we are not joyful and radiating His Presence, then the world is getting the wrong idea of Jesus. Our joy comes from being filled with the Holy Spirit who releases supernatural joy and empowers us to live from that place.

   We just had a picnic with some good friends, one who said, 'If we are not filled with the Holy Spirit, then life is a drag!' Yes it is! Life in the Spirit is an adventure and there is a joy in the adventure you don't want to miss.

   'A child of God should be a visible beatitude for joy and happiness, and a living doxology for gratitude and adoration.'—*Charles Spurgeon*

2. **Joy is essential to combat the enemy of our souls**, the devil who can steal your joy, and get to your health, your behaviour, your thinking, and your relationship with Jesus.

3. **Joy is our strength.** It is important to be strong so we can fully run the race of life God has purposed for us to run. Without the strength that comes from the Lord's joy; we lag in our race, we compare ourselves with other peoples' races and we get spiritually tired and thirsty.

4. **It is the will of God to be joyful always.**

1 Thessalonians 5:16-18 says, 'Always be joyful. Never stop praying. Be thankful in all circumstances, for this is God's will for you who belong to Christ Jesus.' [NLT]

Jesus and His joy complete us

You may have heard the famous line out of the movie, *Jerry Maguire*, 'You complete me'. Jerry (Tom Cruise) shows up at Dorothy's (Renee Zellweger) house and tells her 'You complete me' and she says, 'Shut up, you had me at hello'.[88]

Jesus says that His joy completes you:

> *'I have told you these things, that My joy and delight may be in you, and that your joy and gladness may be of full measure and complete and overflowing.'—John 15:11 (AMPC)*

> *'The Lord Jesus is a deep sea of joy; my soul shall dive therein, shall be swallowed up in the delights of his society.'—Charles Spurgeon*

Have you ever been scuba diving? I was blessed with a dive course for my 40th birthday by the precious people at Lighthouse Church. When you are underwater, there is nothing else but peace and joy (unless you have a fear of sharks! If so, I don't recommend diving). For me, it felt I left my stress up on the beach and I entered an underwater world of peace and joy and blowing bubbles with the fish.

I agree with Spurgeon. Spending time in the presence of Jesus is like a deep sea of joy and delight in his companionship. It is like entering an 'other' world of peace and joy. It is breathing in His Spirit, so my spirit is refreshed and restored.

It is joy inexpressible!

I want what she's having!

Joy inexpressible! That is the testimony of millions, and millions of people who have received the free gift of salvation. You can't actually fully describe it until you receive the gift and God's Spirit comes to live in your spirit.

If you have not already done so, maybe today is the day when you would like to accept that gift and receive this joy inexpressible. I encourage you to pray this prayer:

> *'Dear God,*
> *I know I'm a sinner, and I ask for your forgiveness.*
> *I believe Jesus Christ is Your Son. I believe He died*
> *for my sin and that you raised Him to life.*
> *I want to trust Him as my Saviour and follow Him as Lord, from this day forward.*
> *Guide my life and help me to do your will. Fill me with your Holy Spirit.*
> *I pray this in the name of Jesus. Amen.'*

This is definitely the best decision you can ever make! The next step is to find a good church where you can grow in your faith in a community of believers and spend some time each morning praying and reading the Bible. If you do not know where to start, you can email me at refinding.joy.book@gmail.com.

Thank you

Thank you all for taking this journey with me. I pray that you have found some joy along the way. In fact, I pray you have found a lot of joy inexpressible. If you have not been able to find any joy, I urge you to seek some help and prayer.

In closing, this is my prayer for you:

> *'Now to Him Who is able to keep you without stumbling or slipping or falling, and to present [you] unblemished (blameless and faultless) before the presence of His glory in triumphant joy and exultation [with unspeakable, ecstatic delight]—to the one only God, our Saviour through Jesus Christ our Lord, be glory (splendour), majesty, might and dominion, and power and authority, before all time and now and forever (unto all the ages of eternity). Amen (so be it).'*
> —Jude 24-25 (AMPC)

Appendix. Joy in Ministry

This section is specifically for people who are in ministry in some capacity. Which actually, if you think it through, applies to everyone who follows Jesus. We are all called to be God's priests (1 Peter 2:4-5, 9).

As I mentioned previously, my husband Paul and I planted a church on the lower north shore of Sydney in 2001 and led it for 18 years before handing it over to some dear friends, Jim and Maria, who have taken the baton and led it onward with skilful hands, integrity of heart, anointing, joy and love for God and His people. We are beyond thrilled the church continues to thrive and impact Sydney with the good news of Jesus.

When I started this joy journey I have been referring to in this book, I felt like I'd lost a lot of joy in the calling. I knew without a doubt we were called by God to do this as we started out. Then, as anyone who has led a church will know, there are seasons of steep challenges to face. These often run parallel with the joy of seeing people's lives transformed in addition to the joy of knowing you are walking in obedience in the purposes of God.

I realised I had an unwitting, subconscious belief that ministry, and life as a whole, would go in one upward line on a graph.

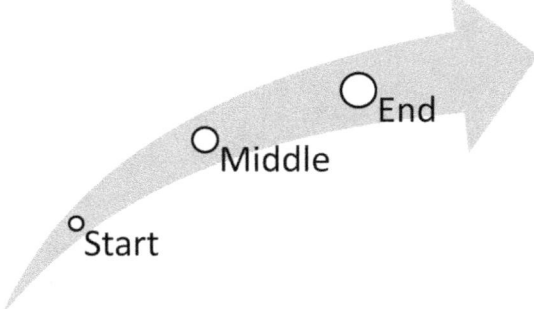

When in fact, the trajectory of ministry and life look like a creative graph with valleys and mountains, and the day to day 'normal grind' often going on simultaneously in between it all!

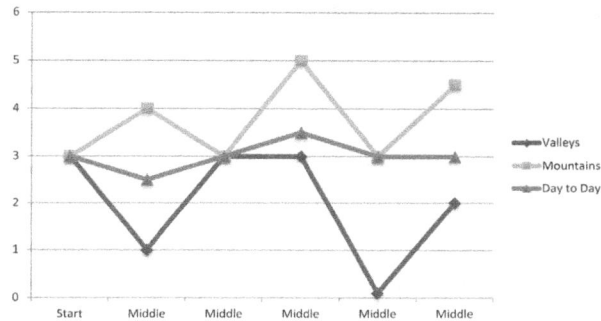

Some seasons are tougher than others and the particular season we faced when my joy went a bit AWOL, was one of those protracted, unrelenting seasons.

Serve the Lord with joy

As I mentioned previously, I started a systematic 'joy' word search through the Bible, starting at Genesis, to discover what God says about joy. The very first verse I read had such an impact on me like a jolt of electricity; you know when you read God's living active Word and you feel like it is literally like a sword cutting and dividing between your soul and spirit.

> *'If you do not serve the Lord your God with joy and enthusiasm for the abundant benefits you have received, you will serve your enemies whom the Lord will send against you. You will be left hungry, thirsty, naked, and lacking in everything.'*—Deuteronomy 28:47-48

The leader of the Ephesians 4 trans-local team we serve on (New Covenant Ministries International, NCMI) Tyrone Daniel, often reminds us in team meetings that the privilege of the calling outweighs the price of the calling. Each time he says this I am drawn back into remembering the immense privilege of serving the King of Kings and Lord of Lords, the only wise God, the Almighty Creator of the universe!

When I read this verse in Deuteronomy, it smacked me with the realisation that too often I lose sight of the abundant benefits I have received. Even in the exceptionally difficult seasons, He has blessed me with every spiritual blessing, in His love He has adopted me to be His child, redeemed me, made me alive and raised me to be seated with Him in heavenly places! (Ephesians 1 and 2) I am reminded that whenever I lose sight of these truths, I stop serving the Lord my God with joy and enthusiasm.

God no longer sends enemies against us to turn us back to Him as we now have right standing with God in Christ Jesus. Even though we are in the days of the new covenant of God's grace, mercy and empowering, enabling presence of His Spirit in us we must remember that we have an enemy and we also have consequences of how we live.

As I read that passage in Deuteronomy, it occurred to me that the consequences I reap when I do not serve the Lord my God with joy and enthusiasm, are a sense of lack; a feeling of lacking in everything. When I am not choosing joy and 'grace recognised', I am hungry and thirsty in my soul. When there is no joy in the calling, I am naked of the anointing that comes from the oil of joy of the Holy Spirit. When I forget the joy of His abundant benefits, I have a faulty belief system that I am 'in lack'.

It's not that this is a punishment from God, it's a consequence of our actions. If I do not choose to serve God with joy and enthusiasm and gratitude, then I am, by consequence, bound in a prison in which thoughts of lack abound. If I do not serve the Lord my God with joy and enthusiasm then I am, by consequence, naked of joy in my countenance. If I do not serve the Lord my God with joy and enthusiasm, I am always thirsting and hungering for more and more and more, without being satisfied.

Conversely, if I choose to serve God with joy, enthusiasm, and gratitude for His abundant benefits, then the consequence is a revelation of His abundant life, the privilege of the calling and the fullness of joy that is found in serving my King of Kings and Lord of Lords. No lack, but rather fullness. I become satisfied in Jesus as my portion. No matter what else is happening, my portion, my lot in life is my Lord and His Presence, His help, His strength, His love, His peace, His promises, His redemption, the eternity I have in Him, my heavenly rewards, and His joy inexpressible.

There is a beautiful old Hillsong Worship song, Made me Glad, that has often spoken to me.

> *'You have made me glad,*
> *and I'll say of the Lord,*
> *You are my shield, my strength,*
> *my portion, deliverer,*
> *my shelter, strong tower,*
> *my very present help.'* [89]

The analogy of Jesus as my portion comes from the Golden Psalm—the Psalm of the Precious Secret—otherwise known as 'The Joy Psalm'.

> *'The Lord is the portion of my inheritance, my cup [He is all I need]...'*
> —Psalm 16:5 (AMP)

If I keep this in my focus and heart, then I am released to serve the Lord my God with joy and enthusiasm, and the 'lack' mindset fades into insignificance at the revelation of His abundant benefits.

We are called to have the same attitude of Christ Jesus; an attitude of humility and obedience.

> *'Have this same attitude in yourselves which was in Christ Jesus [look to Him as your example in selfless humility], who, though He existed in the form and unchanging essence of God, ... emptied Himself... humbled Himself... by becoming obedient [to the Father].'*—Philippians 2:5-8 (AMP)

If we 'empty ourselves' as He did, and become obedient to our attitudes of serving the Lord with joy and enthusiasm, then any tangible blessing He pours out on us, which He does, becomes an endowment, not an 'employee entitlement'. The abundant benefits we receive from serving our 'Boss' far outweigh any earthly 'boss' benefits. His abundant benefits are beyond our imagining, and they are not always something we can tangibly see in the natural or in our time-frame. Then at other times, He completely surprises us with tangible blessings beyond our dreams, and often different to what we expected.

Serve the Lord with gladness

Along the same lines as 'serving the Lord your God with joy and enthusiasm' is the directive in Psalm 100:2 to serve the Lord with gladness.

> 'Serve the Lord with gladness; come before His presence with singing. Know that the Lord, He is God; it is He who has made us, and not we ourselves; we are His people and the sheep of His pasture.'—Psalm 100:2-3

We can serve the Lord with gladness when we know our Lord is God, and we know our Lord is who He says He is and does what He says He will do. If we only know 'about' Him and are not taking the time to know Him as a sheep knows its shepherd, then it is very difficult to serve Him with gladness. We can serve the Lord with gladness when we know He made us and how He made us and what He made us for and what He prepared us to walk in when He made us.(Ephesians 2:10)

We can serve the Lord with gladness because we are His people who He cares so deeply for, just as a shepherd did for his sheep in those ancient days. The shepherd's in Bible times would fiercely guard their sheep. King David was a shepherd before being king. He would grab a sheep out of the mouth of a lion or bear and club the wild beast to death (1 Samuel 17), such was the care he had for his sheep.

The other great news is, we can ask God to make us glad.

> 'You (God) make him (David, the author) exceedingly glad with the joy of Your presence.'—Psalm 21:6 (AMPC)

How does He make us glad? With the joy of His Presence. So, it is still our choice to make. We have to spend time in His Presence and when we do, in that place, He makes us glad.

When we serve the Lord, He mandates us to choose to do so with gladness. When we serve the Lord, we are not to do so with reluctance or with bitterness or with discontent. With the enabling of the Holy Spirit, we can ask Him to make us glad; to displace the bitterness or discontent with gladness.

I mentioned Joni Eareckson Tada in Chapter 8. She is a quadriplegic and a great inspiration. Here is what she says about serving God with gladness, which certainly can't be easy as a quadriplegic.

> 'Serving the Lord with gladness—did you know that that's a command?... Now that's something I enjoy doing. And I love it that the people around me serve God in the same way. Like the girls who get me up in the morning.
>
> It is not the easiest routine, getting me ready to sit up in my wheelchair. It involves a bed bath, exercises, toileting routines, leg bag straps, corsets, getting me dressed—so much more. And my friends all know that when they help me, they are really serving God ... ministering to me, the least of the brethren ....
>
> I do recall, though, when there was one woman, that, she did not serve the Lord with gladness. To her, getting me up in the morning was her chance to unload problems. The minute she would arrive in my bedroom to help me, she saw it as an opportunity to tell me all her woes and everything that was going wrong ... yeah, she was serving, and she was sitting me up in my wheelchair; but her sullen spirit made the morning harder than most ....
>
> But to serve the Lord with gladness, ah, now there's a glorious occupation. Those who do not serve God with a glad heart cancel out all the benefits their service could have won them.
>
> Charles Spurgeon puts it this way. He said, 'Those who serve God with a sad countenance, because they do what is unpleasant to them, are not serving Him at all; they bring the form of homage, but the life is absent. Our God requires no slaves to grace His throne; He is the Lord of the empire of love and would have His servants dressed in ... joy.

> *The angels of God serve Him with songs, not with groans; a murmur or a sigh would be mutiny in their ranks. That obedience which is not voluntary is disobedience, for the Lord looks at the heart, and if He sees that we serve Him from force, and not because we love Him, He will reject our offering. Service coupled with cheerfulness is heart service, and therefore [service that is] true.'*
>
> *Well, Spurgeon has it right there. So, let me ask you, do you serve the Lord with gladness? Come on, let's show the people of the world, who think our obedience to God is only slavery; let's show them that serving Him is a delight for us; it's a joy! And let our gladness prove it; yeah, that we're serving a good and a glad Master.'*[90]

I find it so inspiring that someone with more reason than most to have discontent and bitterness, inspires others in how she serves the Lord with gladness. It proves it is possible. And the words from Spurgeon she quotes are both powerful and convicting. We are so privileged that we serve the Lord of the empire of love!

Not only can God make us glad, but He also puts the gladness in our heart.

> *'You have put gladness in my heart, more than in the season that their grain and wine increased.'* —Psalm 4:7

This verse is amazing! God can put gladness in our heart that transcends the type of gladness that people have in their very best season. In Bible times, the season when their grain and wine increased indicates the best possible season of abundance of resources. So, if we're not in that best possible season, we can have even more! We can have God's gladness and joy in our heart. The joy of knowing God and the gladness He provides is better than when everything is going right.

Ministry Joy Busters

Joy busters in ministry are much the same as the joy busters in chapters 7-9 so I encourage you to read these sections if you have not already. I won't repeat them here but will add some points I have found are specific to ministry.

Again, I wish to remind you why it is important to regain joy. It is not necessarily for us, although that will be a bonus; it is for the sake of the good news and the glory of Jesus Christ.

> *'The Christian is a [person] of joy ... A gloomy Christian is a contradiction of terms, and nothing in all religious history has done Christianity more harm than its connection with black clothes and long faces.'[91] — William Barclay (Scottish minister and Bible commentator)*

With that in mind, let's aim to get to the place of victory in Jesus over these joy busters so our light shines brightly for His glory

Un-forgiveness

In ministry, people leave our church, our connect group, our youth group or whatever area of ministry you are involved in. You will always experience people leaving; even Jesus, the Son of the Living God did.

> *'From that time many of His disciples went back and walked with Him no more. Then Jesus said to the twelve, 'Do you also want to go away?' But Simon Peter answered Him, 'Lord, to whom shall we go? You have the words of eternal life. Also, we have come to believe and know that You are the Christ, the Son of the living God.'—John 6:66-69*

Some leave for good reasons such as moving away, or because it is right in the Lord, but others leave offended or with misunderstanding. It is considerably more painful than people leaving a workplace, since one metaphor for the church is a family and a body. It is like having a part of your body removed.

To prevent your joy from being lost, it is crucial that you forgive quickly and pray for them and bless them (Matthew 5:44). When you pray for them and release them and bless them, healing comes to the pain in your heart and your joy doesn't leave completely, it just may go on holidays for a bit.

Sometimes we may even need to forgive the expectations we had of God. It's not that God has done anything wrong—He is perfect and holy and is incapable of sinning—but is about forgiving our disappointments and unrealistic expectations we may have about 'His ministry call'.

Sometimes we may need to forgive ourselves. God forgives us and forgets our wrongdoing (Hebrews 10:17) so we must appropriate that and not hold on to sin. Repent and walk forward in the freedom and forgiveness we have through the sacrifice of Jesus and walk forward with the Holy Spirit empowering us to live right in His ways.

Comparison

God's calling is unique. He only asks you to do what He's called you to do. He doesn't ask you to do what He has called someone else to do. That sounds obvious and we all may know that rationally, however, our insecurities as human beings deceive us into comparing ourselves with others and often we don't quite seem to measure up.

> 'God has dealt to each one a measure of faith. For as we have many members in one body, but all the members do not have the same function, so we, being many, are one body in Christ, and individually members of one another. Having then gifts differing according to the grace that is given to us, let us use them...'—Romans 12:3-6

So, my advice to you (and myself) is stop it! Stop comparing. Embrace that famous saying:

> 'Be yourself; everyone else is already taken.'—Anonymous

We often don't remember messages years later, but there is one I heard over 20 years ago at a Hillsong Women's Colour Conference. It was a message by Donna Crouch and all I remember is her saying 'comparison kills'. It stuck with me ever since.

Comparison kills. It kills your confidence, steals your destiny, sabotages your unique calling, robs joy, and produces destructive insecurity. You may think I sound a bit passionate about this. Well, I am. It is an insidious thief, and I have struggled with it most of my life.

How do you overcome comparison? You tenaciously seek God for revelation about the identity you have in Christ Jesus. You ask Holy Spirit to reveal to you the way God sees you, what He created you for and the path He has set for you, personally and uniquely, to walk in.

> *'For we are His workmanship [His own master work, a work of art], created in Christ Jesus [reborn from above—spiritually transformed, renewed, ready to be used] for good works, which God prepared [for us] beforehand [taking paths which He set], so that we would walk in them [living the good life which He prearranged and made ready for us].'—Ephesians 2:10 (AMP)*

Closely linked with comparison is inadequacy and insecurity. The feeling of 'less than' is a big joy buster. The following is one of my favourite passages. It is a reminder that our adequacy and confidence is not something we have to try to whip up from somewhere within ourselves. Our sufficiency is from God! Through His Holy Spirit, He makes us sufficient in the ministry of the Spirit, which brings life.

> *'And we have such trust through Christ toward God. Not that we are sufficient of ourselves to think of anything as being from ourselves, but our sufficiency is from God, who also made us sufficient as ministers of the new covenant, not of the letter but of the Spirit; for the letter kills, but the Spirit gives life.'—2 Corinthians 3:4-6 (NKJV)*

Expectation

Our expectation for our calling must come from the Lord. When our expectation is not from the Lord, our dreams and expectations can be dashed to pieces.

> *'My soul, wait silently for God alone, for my expectation is from Him.'*
> —Psalm 62:5

Joy is depleted when hope is deferred. This happens if our hope is in a false expectation, which is not from the Lord.

> *'Hope deferred makes the heart sick, but when the desire comes, it is a tree of life.'*—Proverbs 13:12

May I suggest if your hope and expectations are being sunk, perhaps get before God and wait silently for Him alone. Seek Him, even with prayer and fasting, until you get an answer about His expectation and an aligning of His expectation to yours.

Ill-fitting yoke

If you are lacking joy, it could be you are carrying too much. It could be you are carrying that which you are not called to carry. If you carry burdens which you are not called to carry, there will be a sense of sharpness, pressure, heaviness and a detrimental fit.

> *'Come to Me, all you who labour and are heavy-laden and overburdened, and I will cause you to rest. [I will ease and relieve and refresh your souls.] Take My yoke upon you and learn of Me, for I am gentle (meek) and humble (lowly) in heart, and you will find rest (relief and ease and refreshment and recreation and blessed quiet) for your souls. For My yoke is wholesome (useful, good—not harsh, hard, sharp, or pressing, but comfortable, gracious, and pleasant), and My burden is light and easy to be borne.'*—Matthew 11:28-30 (AMPC)

One day in a season when I was finding it difficult to carry on in the calling, I went for a walk with God and my Bible and my journal. I felt directed by Holy Spirit to write a comprehensive list of everything I love about ministry and a comprehensive list of what I felt burdened and weighed down by. Nearly everything on the negative list was stuff I shouldn't have been carrying and wasn't called to carry. Things like worrying, receiving criticism, and my own insecurities are not actually burdens to carry. They are burdens to be brought to Jesus to receive

His restoration, perspective, and peace. Then I sensed God was saying to me to just do the 'what I love list'. They were all what He was calling me to anyway and were within my gift mix.

Of course, this was a process; healing these deep issues of the heart doesn't happen overnight. But if we believe what He says is true, then His burden and yoke has to be light. It doesn't mean we won't have any problems, but they will be within His boundaries of provision and enabling.

Financial difficulty

This is a significant joy buster for many who are in full-time ministry, and this certainly has the capacity to rob joy.

I can say with full certainty, my testimony is that God is a faithful provider. We planted a church in one of the most affluent areas in the top ten of the most expensive cities in the world, with no savings. So, take my word for it, when you are on the mountain of the Lord (Genesis 22:14), in the place He has positioned you, He will always provide. As our some of our good friends have testified, 'you can't out-give God'.

It's not always easy when it comes to the eleventh hour. I remember early on in the church plant; we had some large bills to pay with no means. We prayed (and admittedly I cried), and the next day I went to the mailbox and there was an anonymous cheque for $2000, more than enough to cover our bills! And that's just one story in many of ours and one story in millions of God's people around the world where He has provided miraculously to those who were seeking Him first.

If I could've said something to my 33-year-old self to prevent stress (and what I'd like to say to you), it is that God will always organise every detail to have you covered when you are seeking Him and remaining in His will.

Emptiness & burnout

When our output exceeds our input, we become empty and joyless. It is vital we minister from a place of fullness. If we are not full of God and His Spirit, what are we giving? There is no shortcut. We need to spend time in the presence of God.

Sadly, burnout happens far too often in pastors. There is not time in this book to go into this topic, however, from my heart to yours, if you feel you are experiencing any of the symptoms of burnout, please seek help early. There is no shame in getting help, and often those who experience burnout did not get help early due to embarrassment and shame.

Spiritual attack

We have a real enemy, the devil. Whilst we do not wish to give him any glory or unnecessary attention, we must also be aware of his schemes, his accusations, his confusion, and his battle strategies. He is not at all thrilled about God's Kingdom advancing and will try his utmost to thwart the purposes of God and hinder God's people. He seeks to rob joy and peace and unity.

The good news is this: Jesus wears the Victor's crown! Jesus is far more powerful and has won the battle on the cross by shedding His precious blood. He has provided us with spiritual armour to put on in order to contend and stand firm.

> 'In conclusion, be strong in the Lord [be empowered through your union with Him]; draw your strength from Him [that strength which His boundless might provides]. Put on God's whole armour [the armour of a heavy-armed soldier which God supplies], that you may be able successfully to stand up against [all] the strategies and the deceits of the devil.
>
> For we are not wrestling with flesh and blood [contending only with physical opponents], but against the despotisms, against the powers, against [the master spirits who are] the world rulers of this present darkness, against the spirit forces of wickedness in the heavenly (super-

natural) sphere. Therefore, put on God's complete armour, that you may be able to resist and stand your ground on the evil day [of danger], and, having done all [the crisis demands], to stand [firmly in your place].'—Ephesians 6:10-13 (AMPC)

People pleasing

Joyce Meyer has written an inspiring book on this subject: Approval Addiction: Overcoming Your Need to Please Everyone.[92] In it, Meyer says—

> *'There are two types of approval: one is from people, and the other is from God. We want people to approve of us, but if we become addicted to their approval, if we have to have it and are ready to do whatever they demand to get it, we lose our freedom. If we trust God for approval, we are freed from the addiction of approval.'*

I don't need to say much more than this, except to urge you to press in to overcome this sinister joy stealer.

Dread and Fretting

If you get enough bad news and blows in a row, it's tricky to keep from dreading a similar situation. This can happen in ministry and it's easy to think the worst based on previous experiences. We know that God's mercies are new every morning (Lamentations 3:22-23) and it is helpful to apply that to our experiences and remind ourselves that the next situation will not play out the same way.

Similarly, we can go into a place of fretting when we allow our thoughts to take off into unhelpful spaces. Our mind can become agitated if we fix our focus on the problems instead of Jesus, the Way Maker.

You may have your own joy buster I haven't mentioned. Whatever your joy buster is, the hope of re-finding your joy is possible in Jesus. Nothing is impossible with Jesus!

Re-finding Joy in Ministry

There is absolutely no substitution for the main key to re-finding joy in ministry, and that is spending time in the presence of God, for in His presence there is fullness of joy.

There is no formula, there is no shortcut, and there is no other path. I know firsthand, having tried shortcuts and formulae. God is the One who gives us our calling, and He is the One who provides all we need to equip and empower us for the calling. He calls us to walk worthy of our calling. We are to finish our 'calling race' with joy.

> *But none of these things move me; nor do I count my life dear to myself, so that I may finish my race with joy, and the ministry which I received from the Lord Jesus, to testify to the gospel of the grace of God.'—Acts 20:24*

If we are not spending time with the One who called us; the One in whose presence joy is found, then there is little wonder if we lose our joy.

Reminders

It is easy to get caught up in all the drama of a difficult season, but this is when we must firmly plant ourselves in the Word, surround ourselves with His people and be tenacious in grounding our thinking in His promises. Following are some thoughts to get you started.

God's Promises

In these times in His presence, especially during times of difficulty, ask Him to remind you of 'the why'. Why are you doing what you are doing? Why has He called you to this? Remind yourself of the assurance of His calling.

When those unwanted seasons come and it seems nothing is going well, remind yourself to rejoice and joy in the God of your salvation. Remind yourself He is your strength and will enable you to walk through this.

> *'Though the fig tree may not blossom, nor fruit be on the vines; though the labour of the olive may fail, and the fields yield no food; though the flock may be cut off from the fold, and there be no herd in the stalls—yet I will rejoice in the Lord, I will joy in the God of my salvation. The Lord God is my strength; He will make my feet like deer's feet, and He will make me walk on my high hills.'—Habakkuk 3:17-19*

Remind yourself in those intensely challenging times that His joy comes in the morning.

> *'Weeping may last through the night, but joy comes with the morning ... You have turned my mourning into joyful dancing. You have taken away my clothes of mourning and clothed me with joy, that I might sing praises to you and not be silent. O Lord my God, I will give you thanks forever!'—Psalm 30:5, 11-12 (NLT)*

His joy will always come. Weeping and mourning endures through the night seasons, then when morning comes, His joy is awaiting us.

Here are just a few ways in which the morning comes:

- when we wake up to the goodness of God
- when we exchange our mourning clothes into garments of praise
- when we press through in prayer and He provides the breakthrough
- when we line up our expectation with His expectation
- with time
- with supernatural joy released into our spirit by His Spirit
- with encouragement from a faithful friend
- when we experience healing
- through the miraculous, supernatural power of God
- when we are resting in His presence.

At the end of our life, morning will come with eternity in that sublime, perfect state in heaven in the glorious presence of God forevermore.

Remind yourself of all of God's promises. The promises He may have given you through a prophetic word, or from His Word in your times spent with Him.

Here is a good promise from God's Word to keep in mind during dark times of weeping:

> *'Those who sow in tears shall reap in joy. He who continually goes forth weeping, bearing seed for sowing, shall doubtless come again with rejoicing, bringing his sheaves with him.'*—Psalm 126:5-6

God's People

Ministry is people. Ministry is loving God first, then loving people. In those overwhelming seasons, we can feel like our joy has been robbed because of the actions of others. And often it has been. However, the Bible tells us we do not fight against flesh and blood, people, rather our battle is against principalities and powers. (Ephesians 6:10-13)

On a few occasions, the apostle Paul attributes his joy to the people in his sphere of influence.

> *'Great is my boldness of speech toward you, great is my boasting on your behalf. I am filled with comfort. I am exceedingly joyful in all our tribulation. For indeed, when we came to Macedonia, our bodies had no rest, but we were troubled on every side. Outside were conflicts, inside were fears. Nevertheless, God, who comforts the downcast, comforted us by the coming of Titus, and not only by his coming, but also by the consolation with which he was comforted in you, when he told us of your earnest desire, your mourning, your zeal for me, so that I rejoiced even more.'*—2 Corinthians 7:4-7

> *'For what is our hope, or joy, or crown of rejoicing? Is it not even you in the presence of our Lord Jesus Christ at His coming? For you are our glory and joy.'*—1 Thessalonians 2:19-20

> *'For I rejoiced greatly when brethren came and testified of the truth that is in you, just as you walk in the truth. I have no greater joy than to hear that my children walk in truth.'*—3 John 3-5

Sometimes, after a tiring, disappointing season, you may need a mind shift with the help of Holy Spirit, to see people as joy.

It is important to forgive quickly and avoid bitterness when we have been hurt by people. Bitterness will definitely rob us of our joy and will prevent us from the second command of Jesus: love your neighbour as yourself (Matthew 22:37-39).

God's Strength

> *'What joy for those whose strength comes from the Lord, who have set their minds on a pilgrimage'*—Psalm 84:5 (NLT)

I've been inspired with the concept of encouraging and strengthening ourselves in the Lord.

In 1 Samuel 30, we see that David and his men came back home from a potential battle. When they arrived, they found that the Amalekites had invaded and burned their town Ziklag and took all the women captive and carried them away.

> *'So, David and his men came to the city, and there it was, burned with fire; and their wives, their sons, and their daughters had been taken captive. Then David and the people who were with him lifted up their voices and wept, until they had no more power to weep. And David's two wives, Ahinoam the Jezreelitess, and Abigail the widow of Nabal the Carmelite, had been taken captive. Now David was greatly distressed, for the people spoke of stoning him, because the soul of all the people was grieved, every man for his sons and his daughters.'*—1 Samuel 30:3-6

It's an unspeakably terrible circumstance. And to top it all off, the people turned against him.

How did David handle it? First of all, he acknowledged the pain and wept. Then what did he do?

> *'But David encouraged and strengthened himself in the Lord his God. Then David said to Abiathar the priest, Ahimelech's son, 'Please bring the ephod here to me.' And Abiathar brought the ephod to David. So, David inquired of the LORD, saying, 'Shall I pursue this troop? Shall I overtake them?' And He answered him, 'Pursue, for you shall surely overtake them and without fail recover all.'"—1 Samuel 30:6-8*

David did three things. Firstly, he wept; he grieved; he was honest with his feelings. Secondly, he encouraged and strengthened himself in the Lord; he found his strength in the Lord his God. Lastly, he inquired of the Lord what to do next: he set his mind on pilgrimage, on moving forward.

How can we encourage and strengthen ourselves in the Lord so that our joy is re-found?

When you go to the emergency department in a hospital, the first thing they do is a triage assessment to assess the condition and urgency of the patient. We need to learn to triage ourselves spiritually. We need to learn to ask what we need for our current condition and go to God, our great physician, for the necessary restoration of spiritual health.

When you're feeling a loss of joy or peace or you feel distant from God, or you feel confused or anxious or discouraged or distressed, may I suggest triaging yourself? Ask yourself: 'what do I need from God and others to be restored to full spiritual health?'

It doesn't have to be such dire circumstances as David found himself in. It's best to triage early before it gets dire.

And of course, we don't have physical human enemies like David. We don't battle flesh and blood, but our enemy can definitely take things away and cause us grief.

David knew how to go to God to be strengthened and encouraged. How did David encourage and strengthen himself in the Lord? All through Psalms, it shows us how He spent time with God, and he commanded his own soul to stop being downcast and to wait on and trust God. He asked God to restore His joy and make Him glad.

God's Love

In Chapter 3, when I spoke of the source of joy, I spoke of having a deep heart revelation of God's love. This is crucial for ministry.

> *'For this reason I bow my knees to the Father of our Lord Jesus Christ, from whom the whole family in heaven and earth is named, that He would grant you, according to the riches of His glory, to be strengthened with might through His Spirit in the inner man, that Christ may dwell in your hearts through faith; that you, being rooted and grounded in love, may be able to comprehend with all the saints what is the width and length and depth and height—to know the love of Christ which passes knowledge; that you may be filled with all the fullness of God.'—Ephesians 3:4-19*

When we are grounded in His love and know the love of Christ that passes knowledge, we are full of God and when we are full of God, that love can then overflow to those around us. If we are not overflowing with His love, we are giving of our own human love which is far inferior to the incredible love of God. This quote is about joy, but it applies to both love and joy.

> *'When the heart is full of joy, it always allows its joy to escape. It is like the fountain in the marketplace; whenever it is full it runs away in streams, and so soon as it ceases to overflow, you may be quite sure that it has ceased to be full. The only full heart is the overflowing heart.'—Charles Spurgeon*

His Word

The Word of God is a great source of joy. The Bible contains the words of a loving Father giving instructions and wisdom to His beloved children.

> 'Your words were found, and I ate them, and Your word was to me the joy and rejoicing of my heart; for I am called by Your name, O Lord God of hosts.'—Jeremiah 15:16

> 'I take joy in doing your will, my God, for your instructions are written on my heart.'—Psalm 40:8 (NLT)

Sometimes we have seasons where the Word of God becomes dry and we lose the joy of searching out His words. In those seasons, perhaps try mixing it up a bit. Worship first and ask Holy Spirit to bring deep revelations.

Or do a word study (such as my joy study) if you usually do book by book. Or do book by book if you usually do word studies. Or do a devotional or ask God to give you one verse or passage per day to meditate on and chew over.

Final Words

I would like to finish this appendix by saying 'Well done good and faithful servants of the Lord' to all those who are seeking first the King and His Kingdom and seeking to advance the Kingdom of God and share the good news of Jesus Christ.

I pray that something I have written here will touch your heart and spur you onwards and upwards. I pray that you will have {re}found some joy through the words in this book.

My final prayer for you is from Colossians:

> *'For this reason we also, from the day we heard of it, have not ceased to pray and make [special] request for you, [asking] that you may be filled with the full (deep and clear) knowledge of His will in all spiritual wisdom [in comprehensive insight into the ways and purposes of God] and in understanding and discernment of spiritual things—That you may walk (live and conduct yourselves) in a manner worthy of the Lord, fully pleasing to Him and desiring to please Him in all things, bearing fruit in every good work and steadily growing and increasing in and by the knowledge of God [with fuller, deeper, and clearer insight, acquaintance, and recognition].*
>
> *[We pray] that you may be invigorated and strengthened with all power according to the might of His glory, [to exercise] every kind of endurance and patience (perseverance and forbearance) with joy, Giving thanks to the Father, Who has qualified and made us fit to share the portion which is the inheritance of the saints (God's holy people) in the Light.'*
>
> *—Colossians 1:9-12 (AMPC)*

Amen!

Acknowledgements

This book is the outcome of the faithfulness and grace flowing from my Source; my loving Father God, my Redeemer King Jesus and my Empowering Counsellor, Holy Spirit. I am forever grateful to You my Lord God for being my Source of joy, life, love, peace, renewal and hope; and for being the Source of this book and the journey of freedom it is based on.

To the love of my life, Paul Zanardo, words cannot express my gratitude to the Lord for placing you in my life as my husband, my best friend, my 'tesoro' (Italian for treasure). Your love, encouragement and prayers are priceless and life shaping. When I am tempted to settle for less, you speak into my life and spur me on to become the best version of who God created me to be. Thank you for your profound insights and help with this book and for giving me the space to write. Thank you for prodding me back when I was tempted to stop and cheering me on to the finish-line.

What a blessed mum I am to have such incredible sons, Samuel and Josiah. Thank you, my sons for your love, prayers and encouragement. Thank you so much Sam for sharing your creative gift and time in designing the stunning cover. Thank you so much Josiah— aka, Fresh Viewpoint— for taking the time to give a second opinion and share your profound mind when I encountered some roadblocks in my writing process.

Thank you to all my amazing friends (you know who you are) for your encouragement throughout writing this book and for helping to shape my life in the tough times by your words of life, prayers and support. Thank you to our good friend Mark Dunn for prophesying numerous times over the years that God had purposed for me to write a book. Here it is! It is amazing how God has set up His people to spur each other on to walk on in faith in His calling.

I would like to honour my Mum and Dad who both passed into eternal joy and life two years ago. They were both pioneers, authors and exceptional practitioners in their natural health field. They have passed on to me an example of deep faith and conviction, a pioneering spirit and a steadfast tenacity to live courageously.

Thank you to my editor, Miriam Miles at M Miles Design, for your many hours of pouring over my words and the exceptional observations and suggestions you provided.

Thank you to Eric Hook at Exlibris (my Dad's self-publishing house, now mine) for the support and swift answers to all my questions.

And now thank you to you, my reader, for picking up this book. May it bless, encourage and inspire you to step into joy and all you were created for.

Endnotes

1. Lexico.com Powered by Oxford
2. https://www.amazon.com.au/Finding-Issachar-Wisdom-Know-How-Uncertain-ebook/dp/B07CGD7V58
3. https://bebrainfit.com/benefits-dark-chocolate/
4. *"Surprised by Joy. The shape of my early life"* Lewis, C. S. [Clive Staples] (1898-1963)
5. https://biblehub.com/str/greek/5479.htm
6. https://www.facebook.com/108765389168316/posts/grace-is-the-empowering-presence-of-god-enabling-you-to-be-who-god-created-you-t/134799213230773/
7. https://www.worshiptogether.com/songs/amazing-grace-my-chains-are-gone/
8. https://www.azquotes.com/quote/1404249
9. https://www.brainyquote.com/quotes/mother_teresa_164917
10. Max Lucado, Grace: *More Than We Deserve, Greater Than We Imagine* (Harper Collins, 2012)
11. Nicky Gumbel, *"Why Jesus?"* (Alpha North America, 2008) p. 21.
12. https://www.biblestudytools.com/commentaries/treasury-of-david/psalms-16-1.html
13. https://www.biblestudytools.com/commentaries/treasury-of-david/psalms-16-1.html
14. Paul Zanardo, *Finding Issachar: Wisdom and Know-How in Uncertain Times*, 2018
15. https://www.christianity.com/bible/commentary.php?com=spur&b=19&c=16
16. https://biblehub.com/str/greek/3306.htm
17. http://bibleinoneyear.org/bioy/commentary/3311
18. https://www.healthline.com/health-news/half-a-teaspoon-a-day-of-olive-oil-improves-heart-health
19. https://www.machinerylubrication.com/Read/30787/oil-change-signs
20. Notes on the Bible by Albert Barnes [1834].
21. https://www.sermonindex.net/modules/articles/index.php?view=article&aid=6004
22. https://www.christianstudylibrary.org/article/inspiring-ministry-george-whitefield
23. https://elevationworship.com/song-resources/my-testimony/
24. https://www.derekprince.org/Articles/1000153318/DPM_USA/Resources/Full_Teaching_Letters/Spiritual_or_Soulish.aspx
25. https://my.bible.com/reading-plans/12289-hope-in-the-dark
26. https://biblehub.com/interlinear/james/1-2.htm
27. https://www.lexico.com/definition/consider
28. https://www.healthline.com/health/mental-health/fight-flight-freeze
29. https://www.instagram.com/p/B_agMuLgoK4
30. https://succeedfeed.com/nick-vujicic-quotes/
31. https://www.corrietenboom.com/en/information/the-history-of-the-museum
32. https://www.quoteschristian.com/corrie-ten-boom-quotes.html
33. https://www.imb.org/2019/07/23/missionaries-you-should-know-elisabeth-elliot/

34 https://churchleaders.com/outreach-missions/outreach-missions-articles/356221-missionaries-you-should-know-elisabeth-elliot.html
35 https://elisabethelliot.org/about/
36 https://www.crosswalk.com/faith/spiritual-life/inspiring-quotes/40-inspiring-quotes-from-elisabeth-elliot.html
37 The A21 Campaign is a global 501 non-profit, non-governmental corporation that works to fight human trafficking, including sexual exploitation & trafficking, forced slave labour, bonded labour, involuntary domestic servitude, and child soldiery. See www.a21.org.
38 https://www.instagram.com/p/CD983EYFFzj/?utm_source=ig_web_copy_link
39 https://biblehub.com/greek/5463.htm
40 "Cure for the Common Life: Living in Your Sweet Spot", Max Lucado, Thomas Nelson Inc, 2008
41 https://www.ncbi.nlm.nih.gov/pmc/articles/PMC3827458/
42 https://www.ncbi.nlm.nih.gov/pmc/articles/PMC3573269/
43 https://www.forbes.com/sites/alicegwalton/2020/03/22/9-mental-health-practices-to-maintain-or-begin-during-coronavirus-lockdown/#33fc9d454264
44 https://deeperchristianquotes.com/joy-is-found-in-self-abandonment-elisabeth-elliot/
45 https://www.goodreads.com/quotes/868414-optimist-someone-who-figures-that-taking-a-step-backward-after
46 Warren, Rick. 2002. *The purpose-driven life: what on earth am I here for?* Grand Rapids, Mich: Zondervan.
47 https://saddleback.com/connect/Articles/MAP/2015/11/17/Maximizing-Your-Strengths
48 Warren, Rick (2002). *The Purpose Driven Life*. Michigan: Zondervan
49 https://www.psychologytoday.com/au/blog/cutting-edge-leadership/201206/there-s-magic-in-your-smile
50 www.brainyquote.com/authors/henri-nouwen-quotes
51 https://www.youtube.com/watch?v=vN2WzQzxuoA
52 https://www.thefreedictionary.com/perspective
53 https://www.azlyrics.com/lyrics/rayparkerjr/ghostbusters.html
54 https://www.huffpost.com/entry/85-of-what-we-worry-about_b_8028368
55 John Bevere, *Breaking Intimidation*, 2005, Charisma Media
56 https://www.careforcelifekeys.org/pages.asp?id=63
57 https://www.careforcelifekeys.org/aus/asp/resources
58 https://www.goodreads.com/quotes/670659-i-sometimes-think-that-shame-mere-awkward-senseless-shame-does
59 https://leonfontaine.com/sin-steals-your-joy/
60 Attributed to Oscar Wilde, though unsubstantiated.
61 https://lifewithoutlimbs.org/
62 https://www.allchristianquotes.org/quotes/Billy_Graham/10417/
63 https://www.lexico.com/definition/disappointment
64 https://www.psychologytoday.com/au/blog/the-clarity/201706/dealing-disappointment
65 https://www.facebook.com/theChristineCaine
66 https://www.joniandfriends.org/

67 https://www.biblegateway.com/blog/2016/07/the-beyond-suffering-bible-an-interview-with-joni-eareckson-tada/
68 https://www.amazon.com/Supernatural-Ways-Royalty-Discovering-Privileges/dp/076841654X
69 https://www.allchristianquotes.org/quotes/Billy_Graham/10417/
70 Dr Caroline Leaf, Who Switched Off My Brain? : Controlling Toxic Thoughts and Emotions, Inprov Limited, 2009, page 13
71 *Darkest Hour*, 2017, Director: Joe Wright, Working Title Films
72 Dr Caroline Leaf, https://www.facebook.com/drleaf/photos
73 Dr Caroline Leaf, *Switch On Your Brain*, 2013, Baker Books
74 https://historycollection.com/hard-time-7-historys-brutal-prisons/5/
75 *Sliding Doors*, Director: Peter Howitt, Produced by Sydney Pollack, Philippa Braithwaite, 1998
76 https://www.amazon.com/Who-Switched-Off-Brain-Controlling/dp/0981956726
77 https://theswitch.app/
78 https://www.brainyquote.com/quotes/marianne_williamson_635346
79 https://nelsonmandelafacts.com/quotes/prison-life/
80 https://www.brainyquote.com/quotes/joyce_meyer_565202
81 https://www.biblestudytools.com/lexicons/greek/nas/proskuneo.html
82 https://www.azlyrics.com/lyrics/jesusculture/lovehasaname.html
83 https://www.biblestudytools.com/dictionary/hallelujah/
84 https://www.nytimes.com/2006/11/07/health/07brain.html
85 https://www.sahealth.sa.gov.au/wps/wcm/connect/public+content/sa+health+internet/healthy+living/be+active/walk+yourself+happy
86 "Think and Eat Yourself Smart: A Neuroscientific Approach to a Sharper Mind and Healthier Life", Dr Caroline Leaf, 2017, Baker Publishing Group Dr Don Colbert books at your Christian bookstore
87 https://www.netflix.com/au/title/80209379
88 https://screenrant.com/jerry-maguire-best-quotes-lines/
89 *Made me Glad*, Hillsong Worship, 2002, Sony, by Miriam Webster
90 https://joniandfriendsradio.simplecast.com/episodes/serve-the-lord-with-gladness/transcript
91 https://gracequotes.org/quote/the-christian-is-a-person-of-joy-a-gloomy-christian-is-a-contradiction-of-terms-and-nothing-in-all-religious-history-has-done-christianity-more-harm-than-its-connection-with-black-clothes/
92 Approval Addiction: Overcoming Your Need to Please Everyone, Joyce Meyer, 2008, FaithWords

www.ingramcontent.com/pod-product-compliance
Lightning Source LLC
Chambersburg PA
CBHW070255010526
44107CB00056B/2471